turely abandoning the effor[illegible] may not appear to be worth the effort required to achieve it.

2. **Identify the way and the "who" to the win.** Here, we begin to bring our plans down to earth by clarifying exactly what it is that needs to get done and whom our initial collaborators will be.
3. **Anticipate potential ripple effects and label them to better manage them: Perception versus Possibilities.** To bring our work further out of the abstract and into real life, we then want to define potential impacts or ripple effects as either perceptions or possibilities, via a brief analysis to see whether or not they are grounded in fact or based on assumptions. On a strictly practicable level in this context, the difference is:
   - *Possibilities are generally grounded in facts, are more straightforward, and can often be addressed with hands-on work and/or management.*
   - *Perceptions are more nebulous and are often grounded in uninformed assumptions and/or informational voids that may feed inaccuracies that reside in the minds of the perceivers.*

   Now, while this step requires a pause for reflection, it is quite important, and should not be skipped with a misguided intent to save time, as it can surely cost much more time later on, if this effort is not made before proceeding to Step 4. Doing the work now brings matters into the daylight of reality, as it will help to provide the most viable starting point for drafting up our work plan in the next step, and can serve to inform upcoming brainstorming, prior to implementation.

   If the above appears daunting because you are not accustomed to taking this kind of pause, *please know that it should not take as long as one might think at first glance.* This is because at our current stage, we want to avoid attempting to actually address either possibilities or perceptions, as that could result in formulating initial, unhelpful perceptions or premature judgments of our own that can deter our success later on.

So for now, we want to stick firmly with just identifying possibilities (fact-based) versus perceptions (assumption-based) and listing them out in an objective manner, so we may better inform our next steps. *Importantly, also know that addressing contingencies in a forthright and concrete manner like this can very effectively nourish the capacity to adapt.*

4. **Draft up and review the plan in the context of Possibilities versus Perceptions.** In the previous steps, we determined what needed to get done on what could be considered a holistic level. Here, we get down to the nitty-gritty, and spell out exactly how we want to get those things done, and in as much detail as possible. Feel free to be detail-oriented, balancing that with an avoidance of what is commonly known as analysis paralysis, to better prepare us for the next step.

   We then need to review the potential ripple effects we identified in Step 3. From there, we want to augment and/or adapt the plan, as necessary.

   - For example, let's say our win or desired outcome is greater cohesion among a dispersed staff, in order to facilitate collaboration and knowledge sharing. In identifying possibilities versus perceptions, we noted that some key staff reside in mountainous and rural areas that are prone to technological and communications gaps. This could create problems, especially given that we are going for greater cohesion, here. The potential for these problems is grounded in the factual nature of the locales involved and is, therefore, a *possibility.*
   - Then, those who supervise these staff in more remote areas have stated that once we thoroughly communicate the need for greater cohesion, they will autonomously take whatever steps are necessary to ensure that they are fully able to exchange information with colleagues efficiently. Their statement, however, is grounded in assumption, as staff may or may not have the means and/or motivation to do that on their own. The well-

intended faith that these supervisors have in these workers is, therefore, a *perception*.

As we do not want for this perception to drive efforts that are well positioned to de-evolve into a potentially ineffective use of time and money, we will reference the possibility—grounded in fact—that we identified directly above. Doing that, we know that it will be necessary for us to build into our plan the means to deploy the physical and human resources that could be required to address the technological and communications issues arising from the locations where our rural- and mountain-dwelling staff are based.

5. **Unveil and brainstorm the plan.** We are now ready to communicate the plan to the collaborators identified in the second step, as well as any potential colleagues we may have now identified as being necessary to bring onboard, via addressing any contingencies we have uncovered in Steps 3 and 4. Invite their input, and encourage brainstorming, as this can help keep all participants actively engaged. Having previously anticipated and defined potential ripple effects has effectively prepared us to address discussions about them, as they come up. *Given that we have defined possibilities (grounded in fact) versus perceptions (grounded in assumptions) in an objective manner, it should be easier for everyone involved to keep an open mind (which we will explore in more detail soon) and consider alternatives that others may suggest.*
6. **Revisit, refine, and finalize the plan.** Here, we capitalize on any good ideas or suggested refinements that have come up and incorporate them into the version of the plan that we are now truly confident to move forward with.
7. **Implement the plan.** Fully prepared and ready to adapt, we can now implement with inspiration, and—of course—efficacy!

It is understood, however, that in work life, greater complexities than those described earlier will be sure to come into play. So next, we will employ an example scenario that resides clearly in the workaday world, with our main character—an operations manager and adaptable planner—taking us through all seven steps.

Planning for Adaptability—An Example Scenario

A company's vital storage area is visibly disorganized and has recently experienced unexplained disappearances of inventory. To add insult to injury, unsightly litter is now being found on the floor of the adjacent corridor.

An operations manager (Kit) has been put in charge of solving the issue and proceeds to Step 1, in a solid plan for adaptability.

1. **Envision the win.** The vision for Kit resides in impeccably organized, spotlessly clean, and thoroughly theft-free storage and adjacent areas. Kit also likes to innovate, and in order to do that, new systems and processes would be put in place that will not only support efficient self-organization of the space, but will also discourage the potential for theft and the leaving of ugly debris.
2. **Identify the way and the "who" to the win.** Like any competent operations manager would, Kit knows that this will involve the organization of the storage room, as well as the concurrent or near-concurrent installation of security cameras in the affected areas. Even at this initial stage, it is clear that this effort will require the assistance of the office manager to supervise getting things in order, the information technology staff to select and install the security system, and expert help from the internal communications and human resources teams. HR will be consulted on how to best put new standard operating procedures in place for staff, and will work in tandem with the communications team about how to best inform everyone that there will now be cameras in the area.
3. **Anticipate potential ripple effects, and label them to better manage them: perception versus possibilities.** Taking the above into account, some potential ripple effects arise for our operations manager right away. First, Kit proceeds to identify them:
   a. While they ultimately get their work done, it is known that the office manager feels that the facilities department's support staff

are inherently lazy, and will do their level best to avoid physically organizing the space.

b. The cameras will require attention and upkeep, and the information technology team may not want to take that responsibility on, as they have already very vocally complained of being overtasked with the work they already have.

c. While they have always been helpful with providing and supporting new policies, processes, and procedures, both the internal communications and human resources teams may fear participating, in that all of this is completely new to them. It appears to be a relatively straightforward matter, but they are risk-averse and may worry that it could have unwanted legal implications because staff privacy is involved. Also, again because this is uncharted territory for these groups, the research, development, and implementation of any new policy and associated guidance for staff could require a serious time and work investment from them, which they may or may not feel that they are able to take on at this time.

Next, our operations manager performs the Perceptions versus Possibilities analysis:

a. While it may or may not be a viable concern, the office manager's opinion on the laziness of the facilities department's support staff is based upon an assumption and would therefore be labeled as a *perception*, as staff motivation to do this particular job has never been tested. Further, history has shown that they do get their work done. Support staff also stand to benefit significantly from the result, as by nature of their job descriptions, they are tasked with following up on both physically organizing supplies and ensuring that the area is kept clean.

b. The potential issues with the information technology team are split, in that the necessity for maintenance of the cameras is rooted in fact and would therefore be labeled as a *possibility*. Their concern about being unable to take on the maintenance of the system is rooted in the assumption that the upkeep will be time-intensive and/or arduous, so that would be labeled as a *perception*, at least for the time being. This is because, depending upon the system selected, there may be little to virtually nothing to be done. Also, vendor support may or may not be included with it. Kit, however, wants to be ever-prepared to adapt, so it is noted that IT's concerns for this matter could require reevaluation, shortly following system installation.

c. As with the information technology team, the potential concerns of the internal communications and human resources teams are split. While legal implications are almost always a clear possibility in matters involving privacy, any fear of assisting would be strictly based on the assumption that privacy safeguards, such as guidance and related signage for staff, would not be included with the system. Further, not enough is known about those implications or their potential remedies at this point in time, and existing resources from the internal legal team could be tapped for expertise. So, at least for now, Kit would label this as a *perception*, again noting that future reevaluation may be necessary. Potential concerns about the time and effort that will be needed for composing, editing, and distributing staff policy guidance, however, are definitely rooted in fact, as all of that will certainly need to happen. Kit labels these as *possibilities*.

4. **Draft up and review the plan in the context of possibilities versus perceptions.** Next, our operations manager plans the way to actually proceed. The above perception versus possibility analysis is taken into account, in order to address any possible objections that could translate into obstacles, right from the start.
   - Calls will be scheduled with leadership from the information technology, human resources, office management, and internal communications teams, in that order, as the type of equipment selected by the technology experts will likely drive much of how all teams will need to move forward. Kit will advise them to take possible future workload increases into consideration in making their choice, confer with them on any potential infrastructure issues, and inform and/or engage support from the facilities team, as necessary.

- Once a security system is chosen and its potential impacts on privacy are known, the human resources team is engaged to begin troubleshooting any undesirable ripple effects that could arise, and involve their legal resources, as required. They will also be asked to draft some simple but effective policies, processes, and procedures that will facilitate order and cleanliness in the space, while also appropriately addressing transparency around privacy matters. Ultimately, these should translate into rules that are easy for staff to understand and follow.
- Then, Kit will work directly with the office manager on having the space organized in a way that will correlate with both the new equipment, and the new rules.
- Very importantly, Kit will ask each collaborating team how much time they feel could be needed to get this work done, so a reasonable estimate of a timeline can be formulated. Once a timeline is established, the need to bring on contingent staff to meet it, as well as budget availability for doing that, can be explored.

5. **Unveil and brainstorm the plan.** A meeting will be held to go over everything in the fourth step. Video calling will be employed for all who work remotely. Brainstorming will take place, and viable outputs and comments from the session will be recorded and saved by Kit.
6. **Revisit, refine, and finalize the plan.** The notes from the fifth step will be incorporated into the plan. The plan will also be scrutinized for optimization of efficiencies, and reviewed by all participants for the same. Once all comments are in, Kit can then finalize and distribute the plan.
7. **Implement the plan.** Having done a thorough job with the preparations involved in the previous steps, Kit, our ready and prepared operations manager, is well positioned to enjoy both cooperation from all participants and an agile base from which to adapt, should any pivoting be necessary throughout implementation—as it oftentimes is.

Now that we are far more well versed in how being open-minded, thinking systemically, developing a workable tolerance for risk, innovating, and demonstrating the capacity to adapt can provide a foundation for our personal effectiveness via agility, the following exercise is offered for regular, routine use.

Try Agility at Work: A Real-World Exercise

a. Identify an issue that seems to repeatedly come up for you and/or your team. Then ask yourself, "When was the last time I/we tried a different approach to this?"
b. For nonurgent situations, a good threshold may be about a week, and for urgent matters, it should be no more than a day.
c. Then, consciously engage an open mind and review the situation for systems gaps and for where potential risks may be, including negative ripple effects on other supervisors or colleagues.
d. Next, innovate to identify what can be done differently without negative effects, formulate creative yet pragmatic potential solutions wherever applicable, and give your new approach a try.
e. Adapt and readapt the approach, as necessary.

ELEMENT TWO
Confidence

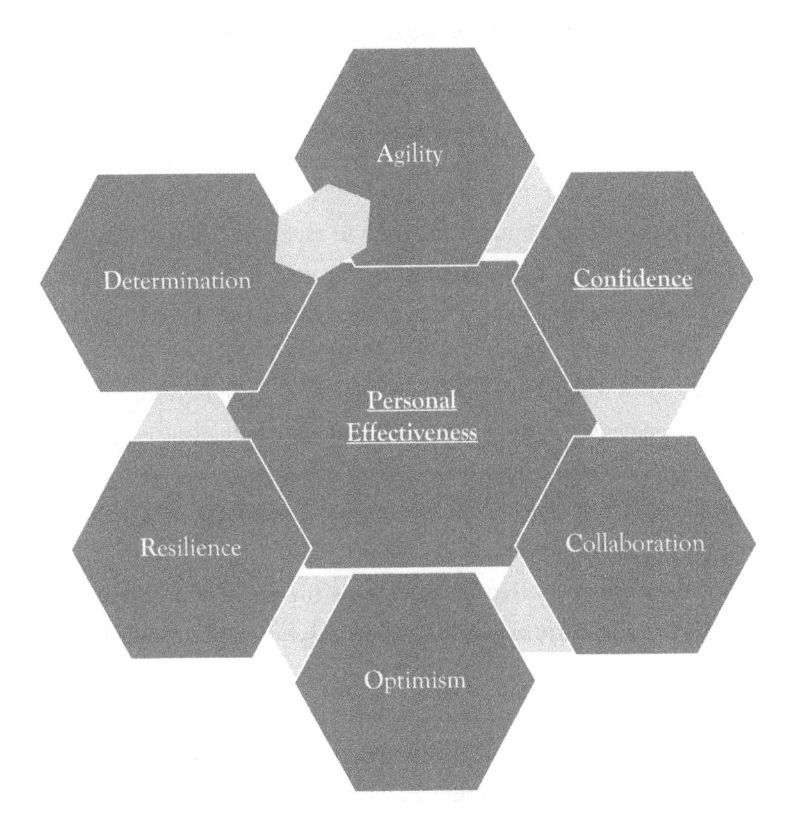

Fostering agility helps underpin a sense of confidence, especially for those to whom this component quality does not come naturally. But we need to be grounded in our confidence. And there is a key difference between simply projecting confidence and truly possessing it.

To be personally effective, we need the kind of confidence that we authentically own. In our working lives, once we know from where a true sense of confidence originates for each of us, we can nurture it into a quality that keeps us anchored through all kinds of ambiguity, as well as other workplace challenges.

So where can we get our confidence from? Let us take a look at the components of it.

Components of Confidence

Here, we will consider how experience, self-worth, education/lifelong learning, and a realistic perspective support confidence.

Experience

Experience can encompass the entire collection of happenings that we encounter throughout our lifetimes. As an aspect of day-to-day work life that has become more challenging than it used to be, it can be beneficial to understand that experiences are not limited to those situations in which we enjoyed truly great and clear successes. We must also consider those scenarios where the win was far more elusive. In fact, some of those more elusive wins may have been enshrouded in ambiguity, initially masquerading as obstacles. But a way was finally found to uncover and extract success—or at least some valuable learning—now all the more valued for having risen to the occasion.

So, the term "experience" takes on a bit more of a different—or perhaps an even more expanded—meaning for our purposes here.

It is generally preferable to think of experience only in terms of concrete achievements, but in our hearts, we know this is not always the case or even what we usually tend to undergo on a day-to-day basis. More often than not, it can feel as though we are taking one step forward and two steps back. For example, think of the last time it felt as though you were endlessly spinning your wheels and/or languishing in functional inertia while awaiting a decision from an uncommunicative third party.

In cases like these, let us perhaps consider the words of Auguste Rodin, the famed sculptor of the masterpiece The Thinker, as he is attributed the quote, "Nothing is a waste of time if you use the experience wisely."[1]

It is clear that experience takes both effort and some investment of time. As alluded to earlier, even as we are now deeply immersed in the digital age, we want to be sure to take into account the cumulative experience that we accrue over the course of our lives.

Situations demanding our attention, effort, and ultimate outcomes may not always seem interrelated, or even remotely positive in any way, but we can often find that there is something to be learned from just about any experience that may benefit us when confronted with workaday challenges.

For example, children are often taught at home that in matters of winning and losing competitively, it can be advantageous to think through what contributed to their losses so that they can improve performance, and then accept such losses with the same easy grace and decorum that one would accept wins. For many children, this is difficult, and initially seems strongly counterintuitive. But once learned and practiced over youth and beyond, it is learned that in most cases, this approach to competition ultimately supports the kind of success that is anchored in general well-being.

To better illustrate, let us consider someone at their first "real" job in adulthood, who loses out on a plum assignment to a colleague.

This person stops to think the situation through, and taking everything into account, realizes that the colleague truly was better matched to the opportunity. Having been raised through childhood to manage these kinds of competitive losses thoughtfully and with decorum has made it easier to consider the reality of the matter, accept the outcome, and then move onto the next thing gracefully, in a productive and effective way.

Digging a little more deeply into the situation, this person realizes that there could even be an opportunity to support the competitor colleague collaboratively, thus adding value to the entire project while enhancing personal performance, along the way. There appears, in fact, the opportunity for both of them to shine. So, the learned ability to think things through, and then move on without expending unnecessary time or energy on any form of negative dross has served this individual well.

Conversely, we all know it is possible that the winner of the plum assignment may not, in fact, have necessarily been more qualified for the job, but perhaps simply more skilled at office politics. In such a case, the experience gleaned here could be a greater understanding of the organizational culture, which can get one thinking about how to better manage within it, or to even kick-start the efforts required to securely and happily leave it. In either case, our subject's experience in gracefully dealing with competitive loss may well serve to elevate him, her, or them to the next win.

Then, there is the experience that tends to come to mind when we think of the word, itself. That is, the type of experience that is gleaned from the gradual evolution of our professional backgrounds.

This type of experience can have a greater degree of specificity to any given field of expertise. There is some considerable chance that much of each activity integral to amassing that expertise encompassed at least one pivotal learning event that would serve to underpin the kind of confidence that supports personal effectiveness in a more general sense. *This can be especially true when taken in tandem with the kind of basic life experience touched upon earlier.*

To better illustrate this, let us consider a technical expert, newly promoted to a supervisory role.

Technical prowess will, naturally, allow for most effective dialogue with direct reports when handling purely technical matters. On the flip side of that, general life experience, such as learning to accept undesirable outcomes with grace—for example, like losing out on the aforementioned plum assignment—can help guide our new supervisor, overall. This kind of all-encompassing experience can not only positively affect day-to-day interactions with other supervisory peers, but may also enhance any coaching provided to direct reports, as they work their way through their own professional challenges and/or victories.

Therefore, our new supervisor has obtained enough of a degree of healthy confidence, gathered from both life and technical experience, to have a demonstrably positive impact on the efficacy of the entire department being served, as well as those they interface with.

Self-Worth

This can be elusive for many, but also cultivated for some, using the positive elements of self-worth, a term which can sometimes take on a negative connotation, especially if taken to the extreme. **Here, we are looking at the necessity for self-worth not as something pursued in the interest of unnecessarily inflating one's own ego, but rather in the context of its necessity for functioning effectively on a day-to day basis.**

First, let us consider that, on its own, self-worth is actually a pretty good thing. If we all didn't experience some sense of self-worth—or even entitlement—it could make it more difficult to pursue any of our dreams, big and small. And if we do not pursue our dreams, we can never hope to fulfill any aspect them, no matter how pragmatic they may be.

We all deserve to experience a sense of accomplishment, as well as happiness, provided that the said accomplishment or happiness does not impede the well-being of others. So, there is, perhaps, some benign and universal degree of self-worth that helps to keep us functioning as reasonable and effective human beings, in society, as a whole.

Now, let us revisit those for whom confidence is most elusive. When properly nurtured—and applied with a strong service orientation— this benign, universal sense of self-worth can support a reasonable feeling of self-worth that helps ground a person in a greater and overall healthier sense of confidence.

Here, it becomes important to consider the integration of both service orientation and proper nurturing, as we do not want this feeling of self-worth to deteriorate into any kind of arrogance, or, perhaps even worse, mindless selfishness or narcissism. All of those negative qualities can work relatively quickly to destroy both personal effectiveness and the collective well-being of any given work group, and, when taken to the extreme on a larger scale, any given society. Such negativity can only serve to alienate those we collaborate with, as well as any of those persons we interface with on a regular basis.

So, *maintaining humility is key.* In a very literal sense, we truly need to maintain balanced relationships in our work lives. Displays of arrogance, or, at the other end of the spectrum, a complete absence of self-worth, can most often alienate others. Conversely, a sense of benign, egalitarian, service-oriented self-worth can encourage the kind of mutual respect that genuinely nourishes personal and collegial efficacy, as well as productivity.

Education and Lifelong Learning

This includes both formal and informal learning. Know that opportunities to learn informally often surround us, and become more and more visible to us each time we choose to take advantage of them.

Time and again, this also involves a willingness to acknowledge and learn from mistakes.

On learning from mistakes—this may take a bit of practice, as the prospect of admitting to missing the mark does not seem to have universal appeal. The hardest part can be the simple acknowledgment of the error, followed by the acceptance of accountability for it. Once self-worth is mastered, however, it can become much easier to do that, as with it comes the realization that the value you bring to the table does not hinge on any single project, detail, or deal, but rather on a whole catalog of merit that got you to where you are, in the first place.

It is quite likely that you would not have gotten the opportunity to make the mistake, had you not been identified as someone who already possessed the skills and abilities to work through it, and ultimately set it right.

So, if you find yourself stumbling in this arena, consider that not a one of us is perfect, and many of those that we look up to have made some truly exquisite blunders on their way to becoming the revered successes that they are now. Thomas Edison offered a timeless quote on his invention that can serve to inspire just about anyone looking to improve their ability to learn from their mistakes:

"I have not failed. I've just found 10,000 ways that won't work."[2]

Once we get past the acknowledgment and acceptance part, the actual learning can usually come quite easily, especially if we approach it with the confidence of past successes and knowledge of our self-worth, as well as the understanding that absolutely no one "knows it all."

As a matter of fact, perhaps the easiest way to remain stuck in a problematic matter is to assume that one already knows all there is to be known about that given subject or situation.

In numerous instances, the clearest path to personal and professional growth and personal efficacy begins with keeping our minds open to new perspectives, approaches, and information, and then applying the relevant ones to the work at hand. Those less useful to us can be confidently released, ideally without wasting precious time or energy by going down a rabbit hole of negative judgment and/or persistent fault-finding. Steering clear of that can preserve the physical and intellectual vitality needed to maintain the healthy sense of self-worth required for personal and professional effectiveness.

Realistic Perspective

For many, the word "realistic" dovetails somewhat with "pessimistic." So, to begin with, I want to reassure the reader that this is *not* what we are going for in this book. It is extremely difficult—if not impossible—to be effective with your mind shut, head down, and your heart closed off all of the time.

Facing each day presents us with the dual prospects of both failure and success. Mindfully acknowledging this can help us to keep our momentum as we broach both our daily and long-term objectives.

So, realistically speaking, and as we learned in the prior section, it can be extremely helpful—if not outright necessary—to acknowledge any potential failures simply as potential learning opportunities. None of us, not even the most successful of us, are without failures, and many of the most successful have survived genuinely spectacular failures before attaining their goals.

To further illuminate, here are just a few examples:

- J.K. Rowling, the billionaire creator of the Harry Potter franchise, had a failed marriage and was a single mom surviving on public assistance prior to her staggering success.[3]
- Stephen King's first work was initially rejected 30 times, which resulted with him literally throwing it in the garbage at a time when digital file saves, if even available, were certainly not the norm. Encouraged by his wife, he kept writing, scoring a huge hit with *Carrie*.
- It could be argued that the much-beloved entertainment entrepreneur Walt Disney impacted our culture with almost unimaginable magnitude, as do the now ubiquitous characters he created. He was, however, fired from his first newspaper job for what his employer deemed to be *a lack of creativity.* Perhaps his most iconic character of all, Mickey Mouse, was also rejected, at first.[4]
- Bill Gates' first foray into the technology business, which was a traffic data reading device called "Traf-O-Data," was quite an exquisite failure.[5]
- Media mogul and international celebrity Oprah Winfrey was fired from her first job as a television reporter for being "unfit for tv."[6]

Per all of the above, the rest, as they say, is history.

Try the activity provided here, and you may see that there are countless failures in the histories of many famously successful people—all readily available to inspire us.

A Confidence-Building Activity: Schedule in a few minutes during the day to look up brief biographical synopses of a few of your personal heroes in the wide world of business. Note where they overcame significant past failures, learned from their mistakes, and ultimately achieved success.

ELEMENT THREE

Collaboration

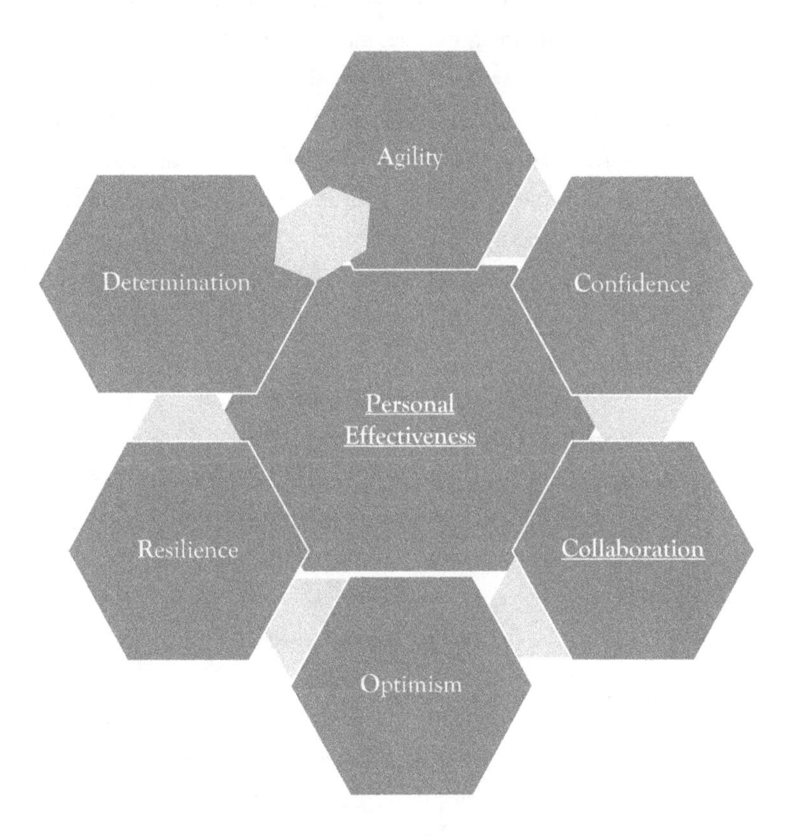

Now that we are more at home with agility and confidence, we are ready to collaborate in a myriad of workplaces with just about any colleague imaginable. This includes all of them, from the ones we generally dread running into for even a moment, all the way to the ones that we authentically look forward to seeing and interacting with throughout the day.

Engaging in personally effective collaboration has even been known to transform even some of those most dreaded colleagues into some of the most appreciated. But here, we need to be sure to exercise what we have learned about being open-minded. Consider that it is very possible to enter into a collaborative exercise with some preconceived notions derived from our own perceptions, or those of others who influence our thoughts.

For example, if one of our work friends has recently described in great detail an absolutely awful argument that they had with a colleague at lunch, it would be rather normal to be concerned about entering into a collaborative arrangement with that individual. If we remain open-minded, however, we are grounded in the fact that no matter how disagreeable someone may be, it is up to us—ourselves—to determine how we react and ideally work toward a desirable outcome. Our actions and reactions are mainly up to each one of us, as individuals, so it remains highly advisable to make the most of them, in the best interest of facilitating mutual success.

A useful tip for more collaborative verbal exchanges is provided here.

Collaboration Tip: Exercise caution around workaday conversations. A small but important bit of guidance seems appropriate here, even if it is something that we have heard time and again. *That is, we want to do all that we can to steer clear of potentially inflammatory subject matter with our colleagues.* Topics that have good potential to be divisive generally have even greater potential to spoil our best efforts at teamwork, in both the long and the short term.

The same can also apply to gossip. Beyond its obvious potential detriment to working relationships, consider that the *time taken to engage in pointless and often unflattering dialogue about co-workers or supervisors could have been much better spent on productive activities.* Simply put, inflammatory or gossipy workplace conversations—onsite and/or remote—are an excellent way to deter both personal efficacy and professional credibility.

So, with those preliminary cautions noted, let us look a bit more deeply into what goes into healthy collaboration, as well as its "Kryptonite," which has been known to displace many a worthy organizational goal, and see how we can work together most effectively.

Components of Collaboration

Next, we will review how self-awareness, group/colleague awareness and validation, active listening, accountability, and ethical influencing can help make us winning collaborators.

Self-Awareness

Whether we choose to smile or not, how we address others, the tone of our e-mails and texts—all of these things can have profound effects upon the impressions we make. In turn, these choices, actions, and reactions can have substantial impacts upon those we depend upon to get work done.

We know that we want for those impacts to be positive, in order for us to be effective collaborators. As we begin to pay more attention to interpersonal behaviors—as well as modify them where indicated—beneficial experiences can occur where least expected, and, sometimes, where they had been most needed, whether we initially knew of that need or not.

This is not meant to suggest that we try to become untrue to our best selves just in order to please others. *The intent here is for us to maintain sensitivity to—and awareness of—our behaviors, so we may reach a point where we model the most constructive ones possible in all circumstances. This is because doing so can enable us to take another step forward in both attaining and maintaining ongoing personal effectiveness.*

Like acquiring any desirable habit, becoming self-aware requires focused attention. We want to become more and more cognizant of some of our most routine, reflexive actions and reactions, staying vigilant around noting where perhaps another action or reaction could have yielded a more positive result. Following that, we want to make conscious and consistent efforts to modify current, less effective behaviors to those that are more beneficial and constructive, in order to pursue more positive collaborative outcomes.

A very familiar example is perhaps the facial expressions we take on in meetings, virtual or in-person, and/or when presenting, in general.[1]

When offering input of any kind, it can be important to remember that our expressions should ideally match the content of what is being said, in the interest of authentic and transparent communicating. At the same time, we want to avoid taking on any type of threatening or otherwise outwardly disagreeable visage. This is not about being insincere or "looking good," so to speak. This is about maintaining an air of *approachability* that provides others enough of a professional comfort level to incline them to work and dialogue with us in a truly collaborative and productive manner.

Along those lines, please keep in mind that most colleagues are usually motivated to speak because they feel that their messaging *needs to be heard.* So as effective collaborators, we want to make sure that they know that we are listening, and we hear them loud and clear.

When listening, we can convey our interest—as well as let the speaker know we are open and receptive to what is being said—via our expressions, as well as an occasional nod, or other appropriate gesture. And no matter how passionate a listener may be about a contrary view on any particular subject, it is recommended to always wait one's turn to speak, avoiding any kind of interruption.

Interruptions can be very counterproductive, and consider that there is a twofold reason for that: (1) it is generally considered somewhat rude to interrupt, and (2) the speaker may have just been getting ready to make the same point as you—or even an improved version of it—using the first part of the dialogue to set that point up. They may have even intended to append to it in a way that could impact all involved in an unexpected but beneficial way.

Cutting that speaker off, however, could discourage him, her, or them from working optimally toward that same mutual and collaborative benefit. Conversely, waiting for the point to be made and then demonstrating direct approval and agreement with it could have the opposite—and far more desirable and productive—effect.

Also as alluded to previously, self-awareness can sometimes be less about our proactive behaviors, and more about ineffective reactions that we can simply learn to release and then replace with more effective ones.

Let us consider a co-worker who almost never makes eye contact—not in person, or virtually—yet is generally collegial, responsive, and eager to help.

This lack of eye contact may *seem* like somewhat of an affront, interpreted as indicative of insincerity to many of us, depending upon where we are from. But we need to consider international—as well as organizational—culture.

In the world of global business etiquette, we know that in many different cultures, this lack of eye contact is simply a sure sign of respect.[2] While this knowledge about eye contact may have been generously bestowed upon us in a routine Intercultural Relations class or webcast, anyone could quite easily lose sight of it (no pun intended) during workaday conversations, and even appear a bit visibly rankled during exchanges with this co-worker. In turn, a look of reflexive and annoyed displeasure stands a good chance of giving the wrong—and resultantly, ineffective—impression.

So, when in doubt about how to react during collaborative exchanges, *staying self-aware and maintaining a neutral but pleasant expression often proves to be far more supportive of effective, successful team efforts.*

Group/Colleague Awareness and Validation

Here, we go one step beyond self-awareness.

In all collaborative interactions, we can strive to stay aware of the potential emotional impacts that behavior could have on one's own team, or those teams that we need to work with due to functional interdependencies. In order to help facilitate that awareness in a manner that will illustrate it externally, let us have a look at validation.

Without ever realizing it, we all have probably—at one time or another—damaged the potential for successful collaboration via an unintended but reflexive reaction during a co-worker discussion. Simply put, if we do not remain vigilant about our expressions, as well as both verbal and body language, it is quite easy to unintentionally convey some level of condescension, or even disrespect, when offered suggestions, proposals, or concerns that we may personally view as unimportant or unnecessary.

So, what exactly do we mean by validation, here?

We know that there are several definitions for validation. For our purposes here, we consider the word in its noun form, defined as "The feeling that others recognize that you are right or good enough."[3]

Put into practice, it means staying aware enough about your reaction to your colleagues' concerns by validating the fact that their concerns exist in the moment, and appreciating that they care enough to express them out loud. Importantly, it is not necessary to agree with them, or oftentimes, even comment, but only to *truly listen* (more on that subject, coming up) *and respectfully accept that the matter is of issue to them.*

Per everyday application, if a colleague voices an idea or provides information about an internal issue that does not necessarily resonate with you, try to resist the temptation to scowl, snort derisively, or otherwise dismiss it right at the outset. Besides risking the same thing happening to you when the roles are eventually reversed, doing so can shut down the kind of conversations that are needed to feed productivity.

On the subject of colleague concerns, matters that trouble or distract someone else may be of absolutely no issue to you, and it could be considered quite natural to want to just brush it off and push to refocus on other objectives, or more pleasant subject matter. Know, however, that it is unlikely that any colleague would have brought their concerns up unless they felt that the matter was of some significant importance. This is an example of where validation is necessary, in order to preserve optimal working relationships, and promote personal and workplace efficacy.

Importantly, for those of us who have the opportunity to manage others, it truly benefits everyone to keep in mind that those reporting to us do not only work *for* us, but *with* us, and as collaborators, too.

The scenarios that follow next provide an illustration of how group and colleague awareness combined with validation can truly support both personal and organizational effectiveness, as it applies to the work that we do that involves interdependencies with reports, as colleagues.

Group and Colleague Awareness, and Validation: An Illustration

The background: Cam and Taylor manage a math tutoring franchise, with Cam as VP of Global Education and Taylor as Director of Scholar Success. Taylor reports directly to Cam.

Like a lot of businesses, their franchise survived a whole host of challenges brought on by external issues, but survived by focusing on excellence in remote delivery, managing to increase their customer base by extending and diversifying their online ad campaigns. So, they have been leaning heavily on their technical resources, of both the human and electronic kinds.

Beyond that, this pair of senior managers can usually rely on their staff of instructors to provide about 20 percent of student referrals that ultimately result in new membership signups on a quarterly basis.

But their most recent numbers are trending closer to only about 4 percent, and their fiscal quarter will be closing soon. Cam calls a meeting with Taylor to see what they can do to remedy the situation.

Next, the two example conversations that follow illustrate two very different ways that Cam can manage that meeting, as well as his collaborative relationship with Taylor.

Conversation One

Cam: *Thanks for connecting with me today, Tay. Sales productivity has really been tanking among the staff, and we need to identify where the gaps are.*

Taylor: *Sure, I'm happy to help out in any way that I can. But I just got a text from Drew, one of our best instructor supervisors. Did you know that some of our advanced-level programming has gotten buggy? Apparently, sometimes it works, and sometimes it doesn't.*

Cam: *Really? I didn't have any issue with that when I looked at it this morning. We need to get our numbers up by quarters' end, so let's table that for another day, maybe tomorrow when we check in with the tech team. They get paid to handle the nerdy stuff, and they're pretty good at it—heck, they probably know about it already.*

Taylor: *Yeah, they're a good team, but this seemed like kind of a big deal. Drew seemed really annoyed, and mentioned that there is no excuse for something like that in this day and age. We rely on our reputation, and one of our best new tutors—who has a good following—already complained about this to Drew, who also mentioned in her text that things have been a little glitchy for a while. Our techs usually don't mind when we bring these kinds of things to their attention, so why not?*

Cam *(smiling, but interrupting): Hey, like I said, let's worry about that later—and get to the numbers. Did you bring the signup data on instructional staff referrals covering the last eight weeks, like I requested?*

Taylor: *Yeah, here you go. You can see Jessie and Chris have done okay—as usual—but everybody else seems to just be relying on our ad efforts to* *stay afloat. Thanks to the new instructor's following, we're maintaining at level—for now.*

Cam*: Hmm... maybe they need a morale-boost...we haven't gotten folks together for an all-hands type of meeting in a long while. Maybe we can do that soon—what do you think?*

Taylor *(disengaged but cooperative): Okay.*

Cam*: Great! Go ahead and work on the scheduling. Also see if we have leftover t-shirts or other swag items from our last event—we can send those out. This'll be fun!*

Taylor *(again, disengaged but cooperative): Yeah, sure. Fun.*

Notes: Through the conversation above, Cam does not make an effective effort to validate, nor to even stay authentically aware of Taylor's concerns. It becomes clear that Taylor is now disengaged because of the known programming issue that Cam refuses to acknowledge—and, in the sole interest of sticking to his point—has pretty much glossed over. Cam never validates what appears to be a very valid concern at hand, and has perhaps even delayed a potential solution to the technical issues involved, which may well be impacting sales in quite a negative manner.

In the next conversation, Cam takes a different and more effective approach.

Conversation Two

Cam*: Thanks for connecting with me today, Tay. Sales productivity has really been tanking among the staff, and we need to identify where the gaps are.*

Taylor*: Sure, I'm happy to help out in any way that I can. But I just got a text from Drew, one of our best instructor supervisors. Did you know that some of our advanced-level programming has gotten buggy? Apparently, sometimes it works, and sometimes it doesn't.*

Cam*: No, I didn't know that...we need to work on these sales goals, but this seems important to you. Tell me more.*

Taylor: *It seems like a real issue for some of our advanced-level specialists. They and their students appear to be really annoyed, and feel there is no excuse for something like that in this day and age. Drew seemed super annoyed, and she's usually pretty upbeat. We rely on our reputation, and one of our best new tutors—who has a good, solid following—already complained about this to Drew, who also mentioned in her text that things have been a little glitchy for a while. Our techs usually don't mind when we bring these kinds of things to their attention, so I think it would be better to bring this to their attention sooner, rather than later.*

Cam: *I can see why this is bothering you. We have a meeting scheduled with IT tomorrow... they have been working some long hours, and I don't want them to get overwhelmed. But you have been on the ground with them more than I have... what do you think we should do?*

Taylor: *I think we need to prioritize this—it involves our reputation with students, and staff morale, which is really critical these days. People get demoralized and demotivated when they think that management just doesn't care. Plus, what if the problem gets worse the more that we ignore it? That'll just make even more work for IT. They won't appreciate having been left out of the loop.*

Cam: *You make two good points—we don't want to pile even more work onto our techs, and if our instructional staff are worried about functionality, that'll distract them from getting new signups. It could also dilute their faith in our product. And advanced signups could want to quit. The errors are our fault—we may even need to issue refunds, if this keeps up. All of this could hurt our numbers even more. Do you know how long it's been like this?*

Taylor: *I don't know exactly how long, but per the comments I got, it's at least a few days. I wish I knew sooner! I think we really need to do something today, and as soon as possible.*

Cam: *I'll text IT right now (he does so, and pauses) ...they just replied that they're going to look into it, but are confident they can have it fixed by end-of-day! Now, back on topic—did you bring those numbers for instructional staff referral signups that I asked for?*

Taylor: *Of course! You can see Jessie and Chris are doing okay—as usual—but everybody else seems to be relying completely on our ad efforts to stay afloat. Thanks to the new instructor's following, we're maintaining at level—for now.*

Cam: *Hmm…maybe they could use a morale-boost, too… we haven't gotten folks together for an all-hands type of meeting in a long while. Maybe we can do that soon—what do you think?*

Taylor: *Sounds good to me, but let's make sure that the programming issue is fully taken care of first. Maybe check around to see if there's anything else online that needs attention.*

Cam: *Good call. In the meantime, see if you can get a date and time on the calendar that will work for a good team-builder, and we'll go from there. We need to do everything we can to get our numbers up by quarters' end. I'd like to reconnect first thing tomorrow to confirm the fix, and if all is working out, we can get to planning the event.*

Taylor *(enthusiastically): Sounds great! I'll get to work, and come back to you first thing, tomorrow morning.*

Notes: In the second conversation, it becomes clear that Cam's validation of Taylor's concerns proved absolutely key to personal, professional, and organizational efficacy, in leading them to solve a troubling—and potentially very *expensive*—issue. By willing to be fully aware of, as well as validating Taylor's concerns, Cam not only maintained a healthy working relationship, but also allowed for the two of them to collaboratively define and address a systems issue that could have gone on for weeks—to the clear detriment of the tutoring staff's morale—also potentially eroding the company's prospects for increased sales.

This illustrates that maintaining a good level of this awareness while validating concerns can also surface needed solutions, support productivity, and enhance overall organizational health.

So, it is vital to keep in mind that group and colleague awareness is especially critical when dealing with those whom we supervise. This is true even if the supervisory relationship is an implied one.

Group and colleague awareness should be applied even in cases where we are informally overseeing same-level co-workers, such as in situations where we are onboarding those recently recruited. Casual or inattentive banter, or any style of ungracious dialoguing that we may feel is harmless around our long-standing peers—who know us and love us, anyway, as they say—can seem unsettling, or even hurtful to those we guide or direct, as we saw in "Conversation One." This applies to formal or informal oversight of both individuals and work teams of any size.

There is no blame, here, however; it is easy to understand how any manager at every level could lose sight of this, especially through evolving and/or chaotic circumstances, such as those encountered in the early 2020s. Oftentimes, in an effort to avoid the appearance of putting on airs—and/or just save time—authentic attention to the concerns of others can often be unintentionally sacrificed to casual brevity.

Also, let us not forget the impacts of a higher level of responsibility—and its companion, higher level of stress—that can come with leading or managing anyone. This can, understandably, desensitize a person about how their speech or behavior might affect the person or persons being supervised, mentored, or otherwise overseen.

Another example could reside within the realm of project management teams, whose work is more exacting in nature. At one time or another, you may have observed highly focused, financial, technical, or scientific project leaders who are accustomed to very precisely identifying what works and what does not. They proceed with pinpoint accuracy—but sometimes oblivious to how one might react—right in front of their entire team of peers. They conduct meetings in this way so that they can hash things out right then and there, and get to the next steps and/or a solution most expediently. Watching them work, it becomes clear that this peer group is functionally comfortable working this way.

However, a subordinate who has been working independently and diligently on a tough assignment for weeks may not feel the same about having open items in their assigned work called out publicly, even if it is done only in the presence of one more person on the same team in a non-critical manner, with the good intention of moving the work along most productively. *No matter how "flat" the organization is or how confident a new or more junior staffer may seem, it helps to keep in mind that many new or otherwise less influential reporting staff may naturally seek out approval from their supervisors, as well as some of their own peers.* That is why it is so critically important to make conscious and continuous efforts toward keeping an elevated sense of group and colleague awareness in mind in these kinds of situations. And if one's lens is primarily financial, or trained on technical expenses, *know that to lose sight of this awareness can badly damage vital employee engagement, which the lack of has proven to have a quite substantial dollar cost to it.*[4]

Active Listening Ability

When we think about the word "listening," it can register with many of us as an act that is purely passive. As small children, we eagerly listen to bedtime stories and nursery rhymes. As we grow into greater sophistication, we take in videos, movies, stage performances, as well as offerings from the metaverse of any and every kind. In doing so, we expect to be able to sit back and have the chosen media offerings "fed" to us, requiring little or no effort on our own part, especially in consideration of the fees often associated with accessing this material.

Getting back to the purely auditory realm, we have numerous and various sources that supply us with a seemingly endless stream of music, comedy, talk radio, and audio books. Some of us even like to passively listen to critical discussions about which of those sources are best, and therefore most worthwhile for us to lend our open ears to.

So then, what can we possibly mean by active listening? Very simply put, it is listening to someone else in a manner that demonstrates that they are authentically and respectfully being heard.

As humans, however, we are (usually) unable to visibly perk up our ears in the same way that some members of the animal kingdom can. *So, what can we do to ensure that the speaking party knows that what they are saying is truly registering with us?*

We can begin with being intentional about our conversations. This means consciously keeping ears and minds open and receptive to the information being shared, while at the same time visually or verbally acknowledging what is being said, even when we do not fully agree with it, as we do when we are engaging in validation.

This can be more easily achieved than it may seem. Tips are provided next.

Easy Tips for Active Listening

1. During the discussion, making eye contact and using body language that is appropriate to the culture of its participants, as well as the workplace itself can let all involved know that they are being heard.
2. When necessary—and without interrupting—reframe what is being said per your understanding, in order to ensure you are all on the same page about the messaging being shared.
3. When disagreeing, take a conversational approach as opposed to a pedagogical one, and ask questions in order to exploit the opportunity for surfacing solutions through constructive and productive dialogue.
4. Whenever appropriate toward the end of the conversation, offer your understanding of it to the other participants in it, and invite their input around what may or may not have been fully understood. Clarify, as needed.
5. If leading the discussion, remember to thank everyone for their time and input, at its close.

Accountability

When we demonstrate the willingness to be responsible for not only our assignments, but also those incidental work items that are clearly within our purviews and appropriate to our organizational roles, we are accountable. With respect to accountability, both our actions and our reactions will speak at least as loudly—and likely, much more loudly—than words.

On the face of it, and in its ideal incarnation, accountability is happily and routinely assumed, providing us with opportunities to be recognized for concretely achieving our successful work results, and, ideally, showcasing them in their most favorable light. When everything goes smoothly, we can revel in the satisfaction of knowing that we can perform effectively and with excellence, and enjoy the feeling of knowing that others are aware of—and can benefit from—our capabilities, as well.

But inevitably, disconnects and obstacles will occur, as they very often do in evolving and transitional times. Especially during busy and challenging times, expectations and assignments can (understandably) go without sufficient explanation, leading to subpar outcomes, even if only in the short term. Emergencies and unexpected circumstances of all kinds can pull even our most well-intended collaborators out of the action, which often leaves the colleagues who are left to do the job feeling overburdened. Unintentionally, this can create the perception that they are now being punished for their competence and reliability. And in turn, those who feel the most underappreciated may leave the organization. Even if they do not materially quit their jobs, they "check out" from a psychological standpoint, and begin to deliver only the bare minimum of what would be considered acceptable results. This continues until they ultimately *do* leave the organization, draining both the physical and intellectual energy of the team, and all those whom they interact with.

So, what can we do to remain effective and accountable during those times when so much appears to be working against us?

Let's look at some of what we can do on our own, not only to keep our momentum, but to also to model behaviors that encourage the efficacy and productivity of others:

- Remember to employ systems thinking, and to most objectively approach all of our work. Take a solutions-oriented approach, as well (more on that subject soon).
- Along those same lines and in a systems thinking context, before defaulting to personal criticism, always consider external situations and conditions that could have affected what is happening.

- If it appears that there has been a gap in performance, avoid reacting with blame, as it is generally ineffective, demotivating, and counterproductive (see our "Kryptonite" tip at the close of this section). Instead, look to determine where roles and assignments may not have been the best match. For example, a critical milestone may have been assigned to someone who simply did not have the latitude or the tools to fully deliver results, but was perhaps afraid to speak up about it because of a less-than-optimal organizational culture.
- If going through a similar situation yourself, be sure to do all that you can, and then be prepared to explain what is required to effectively get the job done. This can help to maintain a proper level of accountability, while simultaneously ensuring that the work will progress.

Ethical Influencing

Influence is very often defined as "the power or capacity of causing an effect in indirect or intangible ways."[5] **In order to be and stay personally effective when exercising our own influence, especially with an eye to collaborative efforts in the longer term, we want to stay mindful of the intended end result for everyone who is involved**. To intentionally avoid doing so can cause irreparable damage to all manner of working relationships, and for obvious reasons. After all, it is highly unlikely that anyone would want to be deliberately misled, no matter what the end result is.

But particularly when under stress, people can sometimes lose sight of this, and feel motivated to influence others with less-than-ideal intentions. The best of these scenarios could involve someone using their influence to convey messaging that is not fully accurate, but they feel that doing as much is in the best interest of achieving a goal that will benefit everyone. Unless, of course, those inaccuracies are unearthed in the process—which is bound to happen in our age of transparency. And resultantly, their current as well as future credibility can be completely lost.

At the other end of the spectrum, some of the worst of these types of scenarios encompass those involving individuals who could be aptly described as solely self-serving, and, resultantly, undesirable as collaborators of any kind. A particularly illustrative example could be that of co-workers who are unsure of their own abilities, and are prone to spreading malicious talk about those whom they consider to be competitors within the organization, sometimes even employing social media in the process. At a supervisory level, I have, sadly, witnessed managers not only doing that, but also proactively attempting to sow seeds of dysfunction among the teams of other managers.

Almost needless to say, this type of behavior typically does not end well for the offending parties at every level, as their own lack of both character and competence becomes exposed in the process. This can generally result in either stern discipline, or ultimate release from the organization. If the manager somehow survives professionally from the fallout of their actions—at a bare minimum—their teams' loyalty is typically gone, and unwanted quits from the organization ensue.

So, the moral of the story is to strive to always *take the ethical high road, whenever exercising influence.* The need for this is magnified, if overseeing others, formally or informally.

When proactively engaging the collaboration of others, and beyond keeping all messaging authentic, also make sure that collaborators know what is "in it" for them. We know that influence used for the best interests *of all parties involved* differs greatly from manipulation for personal gain, and especially in the 21st century, people can pretty much always tell the difference.

Next, a very important "must avoid" to keep front of mind not just around influencing, but in all our activities that require collaboration, teamwork, or cooperation of any kind.

Tip: The "Kryptonite" of Collaboration = Blame. Here, we are talking about allowing a gap or setback to spiral into the highly ineffective—and infinitely undesirable—chasm of obtuse scapegoating.

- Any working group that gets stuck in a cycle of finger-pointing sets themselves up for lukewarm and often dysfunctional homeostasis, at best; at worst, they are doomed to repeated failures. The very activity of blame wastes time and resources that could be put to better use in innovating and finding solutions.

- If there are team members who refuse to acknowledge their own accountability, avoid the blame cycle, and address the manner in a respectful, collegial, and systems-oriented way. There may be valid reasons for their shortfalls in performance and/or productivity, or they simply may not have fully understood what the expectations were.
- Strive to remain objective, and focus on the work, itself. Reframe and clarify as necessary, so all can keep moving forward, and on the same personally effective page.

ELEMENT FOUR

Optimism

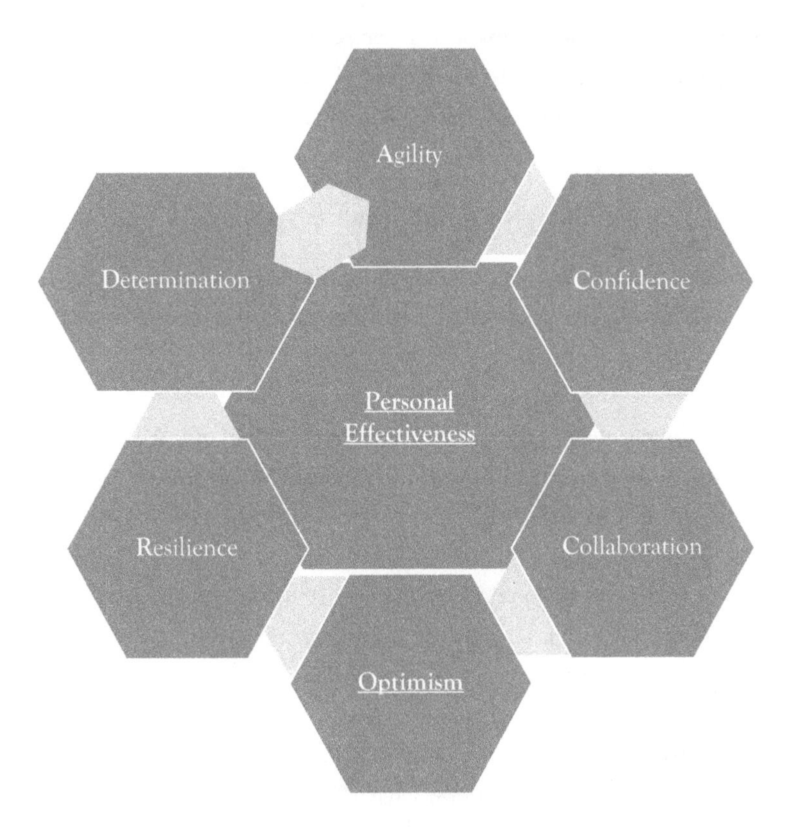

Especially during trying times, optimism can keep our own personal energy levels high, and whole teams more productive and effective.

Having explored agility, confidence, and collaborative skills, we have much to be optimistic about at this point.

While some come into the world imbued with a tremendous sense of optimism, for others it is not so easy. Like happiness, some regard optimism as a conscious choice that needs to be revisited on a very specific and regular basis, experience by experience. At work, this translates to a task-by-task exercise, and the good news is that optimism can, indeed, be nurtured through practice.

Especially for those with less natural optimism, keep in mind that optimism does not mean an abandonment of foresight or caution. The following component qualities should help flesh out exactly why that is the case.

Components of Optimism

Next, we will look at how a positive solutions perspective, planned pragmatism, and an eye to success can aid us in holding onto our vital optimism, and through all kinds of circumstances.

Positive Solutions Perspective

Keeping positive in the face of ambiguity and difficult workplace issues takes practice, as well as a willingness to pursue our objectives in good faith. Consider the following quote from renowned poet and author, Maya Angelou:

"Light and shadow are opposite sides of the same coin. We can illuminate our paths or darken our way. It is a matter of choice."[1]

So, this perhaps begs the question of how exactly may we make that choice a bit easier?

We can begin by looking at whatever is challenging us in a neutral and unbiased manner, separating ourselves as best as we can from the situation, in the interest of analyzing it most effectively. For instance, think of the way one would approach a math problem, and proceed with that perspective.

Then, instead of focusing on what is wrong or conjuring images of horrendously negative outcomes, question how the challenge, as well as its appended undesirable effects, came about, by using systems thinking. Here, as always, be careful to avoid blame, as getting caught in that cycle will most often steal precious time and energy from our necessary pursuit of an ultimate solution. Depersonalize the matter, and revisit the math problem approach. This will help to attain and retain better focus.

Once we have the focus that we need when pursuing solutions of all kinds, it can sometimes be helpful to also reference Occam's razor, as keeping things simple can frequently be the best and most efficacious approach to complex problems.[2] As the possibility of getting the outcome that we would not have preferred does tend to lurk in the background, a brief exercise to help map out a positive solutions perspective in the face of a less-than-desirable result is provided at the end of this chapter.

Planned Pragmatism

We have previously established that planning can greatly facilitate both our personal and professional effectiveness. But when seeking to achieve our goals in the most personally effective manner possible, just what do we mean when we talk about planned pragmatism?

Essentially, planned pragmatism is the art of employing solid planning while exercising caution in a concrete and pragmatic manner, while at the same time always ensuring that we do not become lost in needless worry.

With a focused grasp on what objectively needs to get done, the planning piece should ameliorate any tendency toward a sense of unease, which, again, will hinder our progress.

We have previously covered our seven steps for solid, grounded planning earlier under Adaptability, which can hold some relevance, here. In that prior example, the need for planning and adapting was clear, and quite practical. Here, we add pragmatism to the equation to better validate our plans and activities, which can enable us to best pursue them with greater optimism.

So, just how do we go about employing pragmatism within the context of planning? The answer is deceptively simple. **We become crystal clear about our core purpose for doing whatever we are planning for**. An effective approach to this could be to pretend you are an inventor (on the product side), or a new service provider. Ask yourself: "What need am I fulfilling?" as well as "Who are the intended customers for my product or service?"

The answer should come right away.

For example, even though they are regularly faced with all kinds of potential threats from the outside world, train conductors could say that they fulfill a critical need for safe and efficient transit. Their customers would, of course, be their passengers. Whether or not this is something that they keep front of mind, these conductors provide a very essential, vital service to the commuting public, and can feel really good about that, even when they are having a bad day.

Keeping those good feelings in mind, they can proceed to plan their work and execute on their routines very concretely and effectively, despite what might be going on in the external environment at any given time. Keeping this type of very pragmatic outlook on what one does and whom one does it for can often feed optimism in an unexpectedly easy, elegant way, concurrently facilitating our ability to be personally effective.

An Eye to Success

Next, again thinking about our train conductors, we know that when they successfully meet their daily goals, this contributes to the much larger achievement of ensuring that thousands of commuters can safely and efficiently get to where they are going, and, in most cases, at or about the time they are expected there. But without an eye to their individual successes—no matter how automatic or routine those successes may seem—the universal, collective accomplishment of keeping a very complex system—handling thousands of commuters each day—up and running safely and efficiently could never be achieved.

Like all hard work, this achievement is supported by an eye to success. This illustrates how vitally important it is to keep an eye to success in every single endeavor, no matter how small, routine, or innocuous it may seem at the time, as our individual efforts ultimately contribute to the essential workings of the greater whole.

So, when faced with challenges large and small, we want to support our eye to success by identifying what works and/or has worked for us in the past, innovating on that whenever necessary, as well as recognizing, nurturing, and sharing our wins, as we meet our goals. Importantly, we also want to remember to celebrate our positive outcomes in a manner that harmonizes with the impact of the result, and also resonates with all of those involved. This can encourage a working climate that supports and augments continuous achievement.

Positive Solutions Perspective: An Exercise

1. First, start by thinking about what needs to be achieved next. Acknowledge both the potential desirable outcomes, as well as the undesirable results that are possible.
2. Note how you feel when you think about the positive outcomes, as well as how you feel when you think about the negative ones. Then, *consciously and deliberately* revisit the positivity you feel when thinking about the positive outcomes.
3. While holding onto that positive emotion, analyze potential negative outcomes in an unbiased manner. Strive to stay as detached as you can, but if you feel an undesirable emotional reaction coming on, acknowledge that, too, let yourself feel it, and *then make a conscious decision to let it go.* Visualize it circling and then traveling down a drain to oblivion, if that helps.
4. Then, refocus on the work at hand. Proceed with your planning, and if there is no formal plan in place that includes how to react to contingencies, create one.
   i. Retrace your steps, making a list to create a visual aid that encompasses where systemic or environmental issues may have broken down in the past, and could do so again.
   ii. Also be sure to consider where augmented communications and/or more effective collaborations appear to be necessary.
5. Following all of that, come back to how you felt when thinking about the desirable outcomes, hold onto that emotion, refocus, and proceed with your work.

ELEMENT FIVE

Resilience

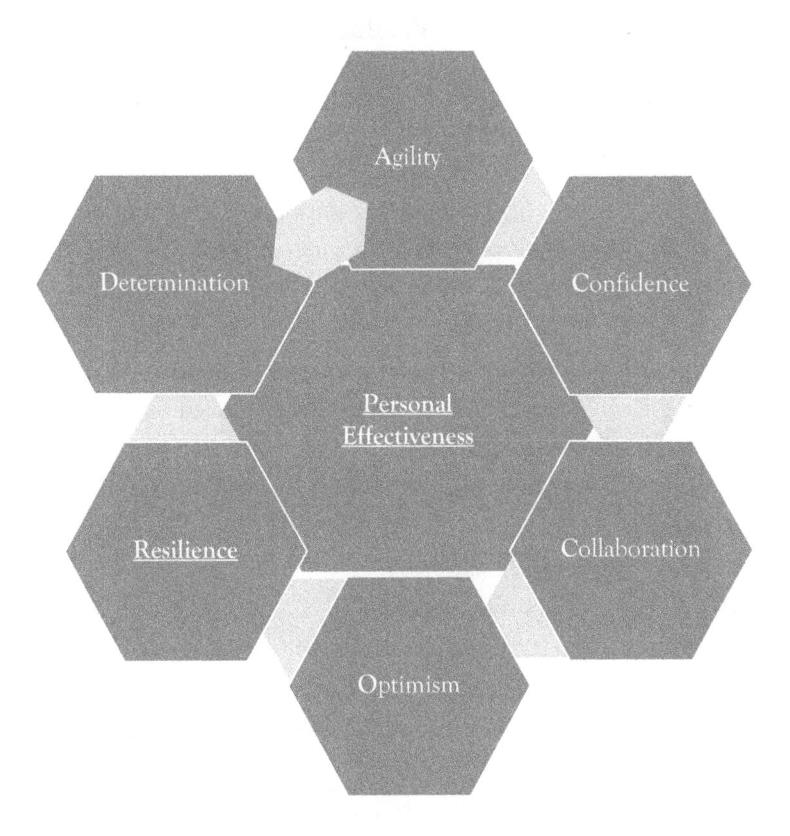

No matter how agile, confident, collaborative, and optimistic we are, we will all encounter obstacles—some of them quite stubborn. We can lose our personal effectiveness, however, if we get bogged down or intimidated by them. This is where resilience comes in.

This section will show us how developing resilience not only supports our personal effectiveness at work, but can provide us with several life skills that can serve us through almost any challenge or obstacle.

Components of Resilience

Next, we will review how vision, a results orientation, personal organization, time management, as well as a balanced lifestyle and self-care can provide key support to our resilience, and overall personal effectiveness.

Vision

When caught up in the mundane but critical aspects of work, some of us can wonder about the necessity of something as apparently abstract as having a vision in mind. After all, when our focus is very singularly trained on keeping the lights on, the doors open, and operations running, it could seem a little bit pretentious to entertain what may seem to be a rather lofty pursuit. This can be especially true if one's only exposure to visioning has been as an activity reserved only for those ivory-tower eccentrics that are somehow kept on the payroll—or even for an external consulting team—despite how far removed they seemed to be from the day-to-day needs of the organization.

So why do so many organizations insist on having a vision statement for what they do? Is not the mission enough, spelling out the important work that is diligently being done on a daily basis?

Well, for most, the answer is actually no. This is because while the mission keeps the engine of business chugging along, the vision defines the collective goal for the organization, and all those working in it. To borrow from a maritime metaphor, think of the mission as a ship's engines, and the vision as its north star.

Vision feeds vital motivation by providing inspiration—the kind of inspiration that helps organizations—and the individual who serves them—weather the storms of difficult, challenging, and ambiguous times.

The same thing applies to us, as personally effective individuals. **A vision, by its very nature, will bolster our resilience when times get tough. This is key to getting us through those times when things do not turn out exactly as we had planned, which could otherwise cause us to feel physically, intellectually, and motivationally drained.** Know that when our motivation is on the wane, a clear vision for the future state can stoke the fires of inspiration, pushing us forward with renewed energy, while underpinning our all-important resilience.

There is a wonderful opportunity for creativity and imagination here. *You are the author of your own vision*, and while it helps to spell it out "on paper," it should be personally relevant enough to comfortably reside in your mind's eye for as long as you need it there. Your vision can be of a personal or professional nature, and the reward it provides can be intrinsic, material, or a happy combination of the two. The key factor is that it needs to be something palpable, which inspires you enough to keep moving toward it, no matter what.

For example, I know of two successful individuals who serve the performing arts industry, and both were faced with what seemed like insurmountable obstacles when the COVID-19 pandemic struck. But they both had very strong and long-standing visions for the future, and both were close to achieving them. One vision was more material (purchasing desirable real estate near the same, expensive area where the rental resided) and the other was more intrinsic (a role in the business that would have a more positive impact on the world). While the nature of the pandemic forced them to modify how they accomplished their day-to-day responsibilities, and the options that made up their visions were somewhat modified by circumstances outside of their realm of control, both visions were ultimately—and very satisfyingly—achieved.

Let us now look at some tips to help us all do the same.

Tips: Vision and Resilience

- Feed your resilience by staying firmly trained on your vision.
- If any part or parts of your vision come to fruition early, take the time to celebrate those, and then capitalize on the good feelings generated, in order to keep the momentum going.
- Conversely, if the vision or any of its component parts seem overly slow in coming along, determine which are most feasible, and revise, as necessary.
- If it becomes necessary to let go of part of your vision for the future, focus on the reason or the inherent learning

in the act of letting go, as opposed to ruminating over the loss. Strive to avoid wasting precious time and energy with dwelling on the perceived shortfall. I say "perceived" here for good reason. Please consider those times in the past that *not* getting what you thought you wanted turned out to be a big blessing in disguise. For many of us, we can measure those times in generous multiples.

- Never forget that the vision is there to serve its author, and not the other way around. Strive to keep in mind that your vision does not need to be static, and given how fast both internal and external factors can change, we should afford ourselves the latitude to revise it—or even rewrite it—whenever appropriate.

Results Orientation

Once we are sure of what we want for our desired outcome to be, we also want to make sure that we utilize our precious time and energy resources in pursuit of just that. It could be said that a results orientation is often more about what one chooses *not* to do, while engaged in that pursuit.

This means keeping trained on the desired outcome—the result itself—even in the face of organizational cultures and/or colleagues that sometimes seem deeply entrenched and thus fully invested in chaos and dysfunction.

To the general credit of anyone who purposefully pursues personal effectiveness, we know we do our best, no matter what. But from time to time, we can run into situations where every interpersonal and business skill in the proverbial book can be applied, and a few situations will still arise where the dysfunction in the work environment is extremely pervasive. In fact, it seems so pervasive that it appears all a person can do is simply accept it and keep moving forward. What is key in situations like these is to know that while you must *work with* the problematic issues—or work environments—at hand, *you must ensure that you do not allow yourself to be pulled into them.*

Maintaining a clear results orientation will support this. It can help avoid getting involved in any toxic cycle of blame (our Kryptonite of collaboration), as the result or desired outcome—in and of itself—is typically not personal in nature. Maintaining a results orientation can aid one's own personal efficacy and productivity. And successfully applied, it has been known to help refocus others—even those invested in chaos and dysfunction—on being productive, as well. Simply put, elusive as it may seem in some work environments, a results orientation has tremendous potential to serve repeated successes.

We know that in the very best of times, it can be relatively easy to keep focused on the results we want most, and then objectively pursue them without the noise and distraction of negative thinking or behaviors. However, in times of stress and uncertainty—as usual—that kind of focus can fall to the wayside, along with our personal effectiveness, unless we commit ourselves to behaviors that will support a focused results orientation.

So let us next have a look at some behaviors that can help support a results orientation:

1. **Defining the desired result in a transparent, nonpersonalized way**. For example, the desired result could be to successfully train the accounting team, supervised by colleague Blake, on how to use some new software. This should be framed as training for "the accounting team," and not "Blake's team," as this can help to keep the focus on the actual function of the learning of the software itself, paving a more direct path to a desirable result. Should obstacles come about, to do otherwise could produce the undesirable side effect of blaming Blake for the team's learning progress, which can only distract us from systems thinking, cloud our focus, and further slow things down. Note that if a valid skills gap does surface for Blake, it should be addressed as a separate matter as just that—a skills gap—and not a personal one, which then can also be approached with an objective results orientation.
2. **Emphasizing positive skills and attributes, and capitalizing on them wherever possible**. It is not that weaknesses do not exist, but as real or perceived shortcomings will not optimally serve the desired outcome, we do not want to focus our time or energy resources on them. It may be advisable to first acknowledge our own strengths, and be generous in doing so, as this can help us to better recognize and support the strengths of others. Then, once tasked with either

managing or collaborating on a team, we can draw on both our individual and collective abilities in focused pursuit of the desirable result, and with a greater chance at a more expeditious success.

3. **Utilizing rating tools and/or methods, as work progresses.** We have all heard that what gets measured gets done, and that numbers do not lie. Also know that numbers do not judge, either, and should never be feared for that very reason. While the numbers may not always show us what we want to see at a given point in time, they can provide a more precise clarification about where we stand. This helps to quickly and efficiently guide us to where we want to be, which is, again, our obtaining the desired outcome or result. Of course, when they *do* show us what we would like to see, celebrate that! It can help to keep everyone motivated and encourage personal and team effectiveness.

Let us next see how we can best pursue these behaviors.

Results Orientation: An Exercise

After reviewing the behaviors shown above, see how many of them you regularly employ in your work life. If only one or none, consider gradually adding more. Then keep tabs on any and all benefits that could follow—both obvious and subtle ones—such as enhanced transparency and objectivity in business interactions, and greater clarity and efficacy in general communications. Note which behaviors seem to support achieving success the most, so it can become easier to apply them to your next task and/or project.

Personal Organization

On the face of it, personal organization may appear to be a very boring pursuit for many of us—perhaps even a "necessary evil" to be avoided for as long as possible. However, know with certainty that *much stress can be eliminated and significant time saved if we can depend upon what we need to be exactly where we need it, whenever it is needed.*

On the surface, knowing where your devices, pens, paper clips, and other necessary job tools are at any given point in time may seem like a "no-brainer." But even those of us with highly evolved intellects encounter situations where we can be thrust into unfamiliar situations that often come with changing physical environments, especially where travel or remote work of any kind is involved. Conversely, disarray will almost always prove to ultimately be to the detriment of personal effectiveness.

Simply put, order generally supports balance. And as work life continues to evolve, so does the evolution and importance of work life balance. We know that there can be tremendous benefits to keeping our working lives on an even keel, and the equally tremendous uptick in hybrid work environments has evidenced beneficial outcomes for both workers and the environment.

Remote work from home or other nearby workspace can serve to reduce common stressors, such as those that come with the traffic, time, and cost of commuting. Within the scope of our day-to-day tasks, however, there can be pitfalls to remote work, with one of the most vexing being the maintenance of two bases of operation.

This can be especially true if one of them is in an area of one's own living space that serves multiple purposes and/or if a shared workstation is being utilized. After all, it is hard enough to keep a single, dedicated workspace organized. If that space is a shared one in a common office or home area, challenges to personal organization will likely multiply in direct correlation with how orderly everyone using that space chooses to be.

When working from home specifically, we now are dealing with a second space, oftentimes shared with family, roommates, and/or pets. All of these are not very likely to have anywhere *near* our own degree of interest in whether or not that space is kept orderly, and in a fully functional state. Add to that the demands for our attention made by our house mates. Oftentimes, taken alone, these demands could be considered quite reasonable. But they can also ultimately discourage the motivation to invest time in keeping things in good order once work is done. Especially at the end of the workday, it could be considered somewhat natural to favor activities that are simply more relaxing, or focused completely on fun.

Remaining objective, it is perhaps not beneficial to consider this attributable to a slacker attitude. After all, for many of us, newly designated work-from-home spaces were formerly reserved almost exclusively for guests, leisure activities, or passion pursuits that did not have much to do with what was done on a day-to-day basis at the office. Given all of that, it is natural that some degree of disorganization will result, no matter how compulsive about neatness and order one might naturally tend to be.

But even involuntarily slacking off in this arena will very likely have a negative impact on personal effectiveness. In order to minimize the potential for that, five steps and two tips for personal organization are offered here.

Steps for Personal Organization of the Workspace

1. **Exercise the power of elimination.** An all-out, wild purge could seem helpful to the mind's eye, but in order to ease into taming one's space a bit more gently, that is not what is suggested here. Quite the contrary.
   - Walk away from the offending area, take a breath, and clear your mind. Then, approach the space with the fresh eyes of a nonjudgmental third party who knows the job, but who is most inclined toward impartial observation. In other words, someone who would not have any emotional attachment to the items in it, or opinions about its state, current or future. You can pretend it is the space of a visitor, or even a pleasant and impartial colleague, if that helps.
   - Take a look around. Are there paper files of long-completed projects in view? Perhaps there is a small collection of vendor collateral—let's say a few t-shirts or tote bags from events attended months ago—that somehow never availed themselves of a viable purpose for you or those you work with and for? Or maybe a loosely arranged pile of old disk files, not accessed for a very, very long time, whose current state is now creating a rather intricate pattern of dust? All of these items—and any others that you see in a similar state—are fair game for good riddance, and right away.

- Recycle what you can. Shred the more sensitive paper and/or disk files—while tedious, some find the activity to be rather satisfying. When dealing with any swag items, know that both vendors and employers will spend real money on items of a decent quality that often go unused. Given that, be sure to consider packaging some of them into your next round of charitable contributions. Those vendor tote bags can be excellent vehicles for donating any coffee mugs, t-shirts, or other assorted items that are in good condition, as well.

  Exercising your power of elimination can not only clear valuable space in your surroundings and your own head, but also provide a wonderful feel-good benefit. This benefit resides in knowing that you have done your best to share something that could potentially serve someone less fortunate, while disposing of items in a way that poses no additional, potential harm to the planet.

2. **Once as much as possible has been eliminated in the first step, we need to get to sorting and labeling, first addressing what we use most often**. Let us see how we might best pursue this.
   - Most of us have routine files and indispensable supplies (think pens, tape, clips, etc.) that we need to easily access on a daily basis. Here, it makes the most sense to keep these items in plain view and within easy reach, as we need to find them as quickly and efficiently as possible. In this case, we can simply choose the appropriate storage solution according to the item's size, shape, and function. and, wherever necessary, label each of them accordingly.
   - Disorganization can reign, however, when we have too many of the same type of item at hand. If this seems apparent, we may want to thin out our inventory, lest we risk giving up needed work surfaces to unnecessary storage. For instance, things like cords, pens, or even headsets can easily multiply over time. The key here is

to select one or two of each that we look for most often, and keep those at the ready.

So, what can we do with the rest?

It is impractical to eliminate the others, as typically we know for sure that while we now have daily needs in plain sight, we will eventually need our surplus. This is especially true for those kinds of office supplies that are still sold exclusively in multiples, more suited for group environments.

Beyond that, there are those items that are quite necessary, but are used only infrequently, so while they are not used all of the time, we are abundantly sure that we need to keep them on hand. This is often true for things like files that are very specific to our function in an organization, such as copies of manuals or rule books for frontline staff that are distributed exclusively in hard copy. This could also be true for various thumb drives that are, by necessity, each individually dedicated to one specific project. We can also build up a collection of infrequently used items that we simply have preferences for, such as larger clips of an unusual, hard-to-find size or shape that are absolutely perfect for an important task that only comes up on an annual basis. So, it is clear that we will need these things at some point in the future. The next tip will explore how our needed but infrequently used items can best be managed.

3. **Approach your surplus and rarely used items knowing that form follows function.** Really exploit the fine art of labeling. Purposefully label and store them in a way that makes them easily identifiable, and within a level of accessibility that makes the most sense for one's own normal usage. For example, if your work requires you to write out very little by hand, but you listen to sound files regularly, you would probably want to make sure that your spare headsets were at least as easy to reach as any extra pens or paper clips. There is a bit of an art to this, and care and attention should be taken, because we want our labeling to work for us sustainably over time.

4. **Tedious as they may seem, go about organizational tasks mindfully.** Consider whether or not the system being created will still be relevant and workable in six months or a year from now. Because if it seems that it cannot work in the longer view, it is rather likely that things will simply fall into habitual disarray more quickly than anticipated.
5. **Very importantly, once you have identified a place for everything, remember to *keep* everything in place.** The first part of this is typically easier for most of us. The more difficult part can be getting into the habit of putting everything back where we first found it. Especially when very busy, it can seem beyond tedious to be putting things back, again and again. But while this may take a little extra effort in the beginning, we reap the wonderful benefit of knowing exactly where to find something, even under stress. Consider the analogy of having to search hard for a flashlight during a power outage. Then apply that to having to surface the thumb drive housing a key file that is needed to address an internal matter that could really blow up within the next hour, if not found in time. It becomes clear that the extra effort of putting things back where they belong on a consistent basis is quite well worth it.

Next, our tips:

- **Organizing Tip #1: Try to avoid labeling and/or filing random items or tasks under the title of "Miscellaneous."** This is because anything filed under that title tends to go unattended for a very long time, creating counterproductive clutter. Consider whether or not these files and items are really needed, and if they are, go ahead and label them for what they actually are. If really unsure about what to do with them, think about whether or not the file or item is actually necessary, or perhaps just an embodiment of a postponed decision. If it is the latter, reconsider whether or not it truly needs saving. If it *does* need saving but an obvious title for the label does not come to mind, consider using a chronological system. If that does not work for the type of file or item that it is, invent your own title for it. It will be for your own future reference, so feel free to be creative!

- **Organizing Tip #2: Be sure to also label or file electronic and/or virtual clutter.** For matters of circling back to someone, it usually helps to use whichever calendar app you find most resourceful, and set a reminder or notifier to revisit the item on or around that date. If the item or task filed there is no longer relevant to your work as the date approaches, it can be easily eliminated. If there are related items that absolutely require hard copies such as older, preserved documents and legal files, consider scanning them and attaching them to the reminder. If that is not possible due to time or confidentiality constraints, set up a separate and secure chronological file that mirrors your calendar reminders and/or notifiers.

Now that all steps are completed, be sure to keep the entire workspace in good repair. Allowing things that need to be accessed to fall into disrepair can drain both energy and time. To add to the challenge, this is usually not something that we think about until confronted with it. For instance, disrepair can unwelcomely manifest as a closet door that is perennially stuck, or a broken-down desk drawer that requires an elaborate sequence of movements in order to open or close.

We only consider the sad state of affairs disrepair can create on the fateful day that the offending door and/or drawer chooses not to open at all, despite our best efforts to bow to its or their demands. Only then do many of us remember that our tools, furniture, and work surroundings are there to accommodate us, and not vice versa. So, if you find yourself repeatedly adapting to inanimate objects that you need to get work done, by all means fix them, or replace them if they cannot be fixed. We want to do this before it becomes a very unintended priority. And remember, the fix or replacement does not have to be complex or fancy; it just needs to be functional.

Time Management

Much has, quite necessarily, been written about time management and the numerous ways to approach it. Some workers who are disinclined to bow to a set schedule wonder if it is really necessary to manage time at all. They may argue that they thrive on the pressure that comes with a looming deadline, often postponing their efforts until they feel the moment is right for them.

And that can be well and good for a select few, but it is most likely only for the short term. Professional experience has shown that in just about every case of deliberate procrastination, the objective or assignment may have been "completed" to a very minimal standard, requiring revision at the very next opportunity. To borrow from an old cooking metaphor, poor management of time in the kitchen will yield cakes that are only half-baked.

So, if it appears that most to all of the day has vaporized while progress toward the desired objective seems more and more distant, the opportunity may be ripe to surface some time management techniques that resonate authentically with you. Happily, a very quick web search should turn up a lot of information on the topic, from which the approach that seems most relevant to each individual can then be chosen.

To help get started on that, provided here is a handy time management checklist, including suggestions on what we can do to stay most time-effective in some real-world situations.

Time Management Checklist

✓ **Prioritize, and to assist with that, enlist the kind of support that suits you best.** For some, that is still writing things out by hand in an old-fashioned paper-based planner. For others, this could be employing a collection of strategically placed sticky notes, mapped in a manner that suits the sequencing of the work to be done. More currently, it may involve electronic assistance, such as a calendar app of choice, along with the kinds of notifications that complement the work style of the individual, and the work environment itself. No matter which is chosen, it can keep you and your schedule on track.

- ✓ **If interruptions are an issue, help keep them at bay by turning off all forms of notifiers**. This applies to all notifications that are not absolutely essential, while working on a high-priority and/or time-sensitive task. Once there is a break, re-evaluate the necessity for each one of the notifiers being used to determine whether or not they need to be there in the first place. For example, consider whether or not a notifier is really necessary for appointments that are routinely social in nature. Most of us realize that we are very unlikely to forget these commitments because they are something that we look forward to—as well as show up for—on a regular basis.
- ✓ **Reconsider scheduling that meeting**. Too many meetings of any kind can cause time to escape us, never to be recaptured in any form. Before scheduling that meeting—virtual or otherwise—ask yourself if the matter at hand is something that could be just as well handled with a well-worded text, e-mail, or even a quick call to the key person involved. If it turns out that the meeting is still needed once that is done, know that you have not wasted your time. This is because taking that step can help you to refine your agenda, which will surely save time in the longer run of the meeting itself. Also, once it is determined that a meeting will, in fact, be necessary, stick to the timeframe originally allotted for it, and respectfully rein in any conversations that circle, or discussions that otherwise appear to be heading toward unproductive tangents.

Some help for that, next:

- In the case of circling conversations, it may be most advisable to simply but politely state that the conversation is doing just that—circling—and recommend that the meeting move on, so that the subject can be further explored on an individual basis. Giving the subject a little more time and offline thought can help to determine why the discussion appeared unable to progress in its current state. If that cuts the meeting short, consider that it is quite possible that most colleagues may be very happy about getting out of a meeting early. It can also help to invite attendees' suggestions for solutions, to be applied next time.
- In case of discussions that are becoming unproductively tangential, validation can be employed. Make it clear that the speaker is being actively listened to, for example, "That sounds like a solid idea—let's follow up on that offline after today's meeting." Then, be sure to follow up, as promised. This will help to maintain the working relationship as an effectively collaborative one. Also consider that there could be a kernel of true genius embedded in that tangent that will help everyone get to a needed outcome, and in a manner that is significantly better and much faster. But we will never allow that beneficial outcome to occur unless we invest the relatively shorter period of time it takes to have—and manage—the conversation, in the first place.

✓ **On the subject of e-mail—and this goes for paper mail and other documents, as well—employ simple organization techniques, much like the ones addressed earlier**. Use folders, electronic or otherwise, and, importantly, do all you can to try to touch each document once, and once only. For correspondence that requires revisiting, prioritize, organize, and track accordingly, also as addressed earlier. If that is done regularly—or better yet, habitually—that correspondence will be readily available when comes the time for it to resurface for that all-important follow-up. Zero time should be lost, because you will know exactly where that correspondence is, and precisely where you left off with it.

✓ **Finally, if an inclination to procrastinate crops up—like it does for so many of us—it can be extremely beneficial to consciously monitor it.** Just being mindful of the fact that we are procrastinating can assist in ameliorating the problem.

- For example, we may catch ourselves delaying progress by repeatedly taking "click bait." We can fall into a rabbit hole of what we started off thinking was going to be useful information, and then somehow wound up visiting our third round of social media influencers, or even stuck in an entertainment or gaming vortex. If this happens, employ mindfulness, and *acknowledge that it is simply time to stop*. Then, *be sure to actually stop*. If that seems too extreme in the moment, use the calendaring skills as discussed earlier and get "Internet Fun Time" on the schedule. This can help to effectively progress our work, without creating a feeling of being cheated out of some of our favorite distractions. Importantly, when we choose to put fun time on the calendar, we want to make note of the estimated amount of time allowed for it, as the practice of consciously setting a limit can help us commit to stopping on time. This can take a bit of practice, but if we keep at it, the long-term benefit of time saved and recovered can far outweigh the effort required.

Balanced Lifestyle and Self-Care

The events of the early 2020s have clearly illustrated the critical importance of both physical and psychological health. There is no doubt that taking action in the interest of desirable results is necessary, but we must keep in mind that the instrument that engages in that action has to be in good working order.

As one cannot play a proper—or even listenable—composition on a musical instrument that is broken, or even somewhat out of tune, we cannot expect our own bodies and minds to produce good work when either or both of them are badly in need of attention and/or rest.

Fortunately, both our bodies and minds are, in most cases, well equipped to send out clear signals to us when rest and attention are needed. Physically, this can oftentimes take the form of mild pain or tiredness. When our minds are getting a bit weary, we may notice a bit of unnavigable brain fog. Here, it is exceedingly important to remain open to and respectful of those signals, because if we do not, it is rather likely that they may become more and more pronounced over time. This can lead to various kinds of maladies that may negatively impact our work, our health, and therefore our personal effectiveness.

So, it is clear that we must remain openly receptive to the signals that our bodies and minds send us, in the best interest of our self-care, and the maintenance of a balanced lifestyle.

Like many other attributes, this kind of very personal openness comes more naturally to some than to others. If accustomed to ignoring pain or mental exhaustion, it is difficult to acknowledge the importance of these physical and mental signposts, especially if we are culturally predisposed to do that, and/or if we have been taught to simply shrug them off in the interest of supporting what is believed to be an acceptable work ethic.

However, to do that could be a very regrettable mistake, as we know that it can prove virtually impossible to effectively produce acceptable work if one's health is out of order. Beyond the previously mentioned predispositions to overtaxing oneself, those of us who are especially inspired by our current aspirations may sometimes let these signals fall by the wayside, with the notion of completing an ambitious task that is related to a passion project.

But here again, the quality of the work output is quite likely to suffer. In the interest of remaining personally effective, we know that this is not advisable, especially if we continue to push those signals off of our radar for too long. Both physical and psychological health could become very seriously at stake.

In tandem with supporting our ability to keep an open mind as alluded to earlier under Agility, developing a habitual practice of mindfulness, even taken on its own, can also provide an especially sturdy support for our resilience in the long run.

For those unfamiliar with the term, the Cambridge Dictionary online defines mindfulness as "the practice of being aware of your body, mind and feelings in the present moment, thought to create a feeling of calm."[1]

It is also thought that depression and anxiety can be somewhat relieved through the practice of mindfulness.

An apt bit of layman's guidance on the subject is offered by *Time Magazine*:

"Mindfulness is not about getting anywhere else—it's about being where you are and knowing it."[2]

It is also worth noting that the effort to become more mindful bears no cost, yet it can offer much in return as an adaptable foundational support for maintaining a balanced lifestyle, as well as facilitating self-care.

By now, we are pretty sure that to put one's best foot forward toward personal effectiveness, that foot needs a good, strong, and—ideally—flexible foundation. This is especially true in matters around resilience, as resilience itself implies a need to "bounce back." When this bouncing back inevitably becomes necessary, that core will prove to be something that is both responsive and solid to land upon. So, we want to develop solid routines and good, holistic lifestyle habits that support a flexible yet reliable physical and psychological core within ourselves.

But what may those routines and habits look like in real life?

As diverse as we are as human beings, they are going to look a little bit different for everyone. At their nucleus, however, we can often find similarities, with some suggestions offered for easy reference, here.

Routines for Resilience

- **Routines that support the maintenance of order.** As touched upon earlier, we may all have differing notions—and therefore, manifestations—of what order really looks like, and what we want to do to maintain it with consistency. For some, this could mean a daily, scheduled window of time set aside for tidying up and organizing, as brief or as long as any given individual needs for it to be. For others, it could be a longer scheduled time, but on a weekly basis, with perhaps a monthly catch-up planned and dedicated to those tasks that proved a bit too elusive to tackle during the week. And what about those of us who tend to avoid these kinds of activities at all costs? Our avoiders could perhaps invest just a few minutes per day of cleaning and straightening up—best done before starting anything else—practicing the notion that it can prove easier to do what one hates to do first, thus clearing the rest of the day for activities that are more enjoyable.

  In all cases, it is most critical that the end result for each individual and unique person is a sense of order that is not only visible, but can be felt palpably in one's immediate surroundings. This is key, as it may serve as a springboard to the strong sense of clarity needed to be most effective both within our surroundings, and in the outside and/or virtual world.
- **Making healthful food and drink choices on a routine basis.** Here, it is important to really know yourself, and choose what is right for you. Note that your choices do not have to necessarily be those proscribed products and menu items that are target-marketed to the ubiquitous "health" segment, as what seems to be very beneficial for one person may turn out to be borderline toxic for someone else. How to tell the difference? Know your body, and consult with your doctor or other medical professional. Consider

carefully any conditions that you are managing, and note what the potential impacts could be of what you choose to consume. Then, of course, consume healthfully and mindfully. Note how you feel the next time after taking in the kinds of things that you generally choose to eat and drink on a regular basis. *Pay real attention to how you react.* If those choices leave you feeling more fit, vibrant, and alive, then it is very possible that those could be good choices for you. Conversely, if they make you feel sloppy, sluggish, depleted, or sick in any way, then the direct opposite may very likely be true. Paying real attention to what we eat and drink, and then objectively noting the way we feel later on can be pivotal in supporting our efforts to make beneficial, healthful choices on a habitual basis.

- **Physical and mental exercise, practiced as a desired habit.** We all know what exercise is, and the myriad of forms it can take, for both our bodies and our brains. The key here is to identify things that we really like to do—and that are also advisable for our current physical and mental state. Then, we want to do them on a truly regular basis, proceeding with a schedule that suits both our timetables and our capabilities. To do otherwise can be a real recipe for failure, as it is simply too easy to avoid these activities.

  Very importantly, and as with what we choose to eat, drink, or otherwise consume, it can be best to consult with your doctor about this. When initially approaching the very idea of exercise, some of us can tend to aim either too high or too low. If a physical or mental pursuit is too easy, it may become very boring very quickly, and thus more likely to be avoided. Conversely, if the tasks identified are too difficult, this is problematic, too. Injury is an obvious risk. On the less extreme end, if no desirable short-term outcomes are realistically viable, this could leave a person feeling defeated right at the outset, encouraging undesirable avoidance.

  Creating challenges for the sake of challenge itself can also prove counterproductive. For example, you may really enjoy yoga and have reaped some benefits from it, but outside influences and/or a nagging inner critic suggests that yoga is no longer enough, and marathon training should now be pursued. Strive to brush those unwanted influences aside and allow yourself the time and space for your workout of choice, once confirmed that it is healthful for you.

On the more cranial side, if you find word puzzles fun and entertaining, but something or someone either inside or outside of yourself is hammering on the virtues of learning a difficult new language, keep on with the word puzzles, and let yourself enjoy them. It is not necessary—or usually even viable—to try and please a tyrannical inner boss, or live up to someone else's ideal of what is right for you. If, at some point in the future you believe that you may want to actually learn a foreign tongue, go for one that you find the most appealing, as well as most doable on a regular basis, the same way you would with any of your other cranial workouts. And by all means, reading or indulging in your favorite audiobooks or educational programming can prove very refreshing. What you can gain intellectually via these seemingly passive activities may pleasantly surprise you.

- **Downtime, as part of the daily routine.** Otherwise often known as "me time," these are the moments we set aside to do something on our own to clear the mind and recharge the body. This can mean meditating (as we covered earlier in this book), strumming a guitar, or just listening to music. We may like enjoy going to the driving range, reading or watching something that provides some healthy escapism, or any other relaxing, rejuvenating, healthful activity one may choose. Note that it does not have to be the same activity each day, and as a matter of fact, if you find that you are more inclined to maintain your downtime when you mix things up, then by all means, do so. As usual, the most important factor is that you remember to take a little time to recharge on a consistent basis.

- **Habitually choosing happiness.** The very young may tend to believe that happiness is something beatifically bestowed upon us from the outside. But those of us who have been out in the world for a while know that happiness requires effort, especially when there is a lot of negativity around. And the more experienced of us also may know that while we would generally prefer to keep only positive people around us, that is just not always possible.

  It can be doubly difficult to keep a chin up when a colleague seems to be on a never-ending fault-finding rant, and the temptation can sometimes be strong to join in and get on that road to nowhere with them, if only in the hopes that your willingness to agree with their naysaying will calm their complaints. Know that you would be well served to avoid doing that, however, because quite often, your agreement with their sour outlook may only fan the flames of their discontent, and very likely send you spiraling into their undesirable, unproductive, and ineffective mindset.

  So, on a daily basis and wherever possible, remind yourself that except for the most dire of circumstances and situations, the option for choosing happiness is usually there. It often proves to be the most beneficial choice. Also—unless it is completely inappropriate to what is going on in the moment—choose to smile, as well. This is because the very act of smiling has been known to not only lift one's mood, but to also buoy the outlook of those around us.
- **Practicing gratitude on a regular basis.** While most of us know in our hearts that we have much to be grateful for, we do not always make it a point to acknowledge that gratitude consciously, and on a regular basis. No matter how frequently one might choose to do so, consider that the time and effort investment for doing this is miniscule, but the payoff in good feelings alone can be truly colossal. Give it a try the next time you are feeling down.
- **Scheduling quality time with people whose company you sincerely enjoy.** These may be friends and/or family

members, or even members of a club that you enjoy interacting with. The key factor here is that the time is, in fact, enjoyable, and the time spent together leaves you with good feelings about them. Like many of us, if you find yourself meeting up with a specific person that consistently leaves you rather drained of energy and less happy with your worldview than when before you saw them, reconsider how much time is spent with them, and how frequently you do connect. You may not want to toss them out of your life completely, especially if there is a history of camaraderie there. It may just be time to give them a little reprieve, and consider other options for time spent socially for the time being.

Good feelings can tend to beget more of them, as well as the vital energy needed to stay effective. So, keeping company with those who demonstrate a positive demeanor and the mutual respect that often goes with it can most often serve to support an effectively balanced lifestyle.

- **Engage in a spiritual practice of choice, as it applies to you.** This one is rather self-explanatory. I had an acquaintance who sometimes said during challenging times, "I need a little bit of church today," and by doing so, it somehow always seemed to provide her a world of good. On the flip side of that, I have a few friends whose collective faith thrives in the mysteries of the cosmos, and when things get tough, that is where they escape to, whether by virtual or actual reality. It truly seems to help them get their drive and determination back. There are no judgments in keeping an open heart to believing in something abstract but positive, as long as it does not pose any harm to yourself or anyone else. Doing so can be extremely helpful to preserving energy, and supporting personal efficacy in the mundane.
- **Getting enough quality rest.** This is a matter that can come up in casual conversations somewhat frequently, especially on those days when friends or colleagues feel that their sleep time has been inadequate. And after many years of being part of those conversations, I can

anecdotally but rather confidently report that the amount of quality rest needed by those individuals spoken to can range at anywhere from 5 to 10 hours per sleep cycle, whether that sleep cycle was nocturnal or not.

Opinions about napping really ran the gamut as well, but with most agreeing it could be a good idea for some folks. The one universal commonality was that "enough" quality rest has to be defined by each individual, and very authentically so. If still feeling tired after 5 hours of shuteye, but mired in a cloud of lethargy after 9 or 10, consider that your sleeping sweet spot could be somewhere in between those two numbers. And, let's not forget about the napping option, especially for those who are challenged to get more than a few solid hours of sleep at a time.

Next, now that we know a bit more about how to keep ourselves cared for and balanced in the interest of resilience, following is a tip for those times when faced with difficult but unavoidable interactions with others who perhaps value balance—and balanced, effective discourse—noticeably less.

Keeping Cool and Effective in the Midst of Hot-Headedness: A Resilience Tip

When circumstances hit us with unexpected and unwanted results, heated discussions can ensue which threaten to undermine not only vital energy and resources, but all progress made and lessons learned so far. Avoid getting pulled into the fray.

If you cannot physically stay out of the way of dysfunctional discourse, then stop, take a breath, and do your best to bring everyone's focus concretely back to the actual work at hand, especially if blame is in the air. Give yourself a break, as they say, and when the opportunity presents itself, respectfully suggest that the others do the same. Model your own personal effectiveness to help keep everyone's eyes on the prize, and see how colleagues can, indeed, follow suit.

ELEMENT SIX

Determination

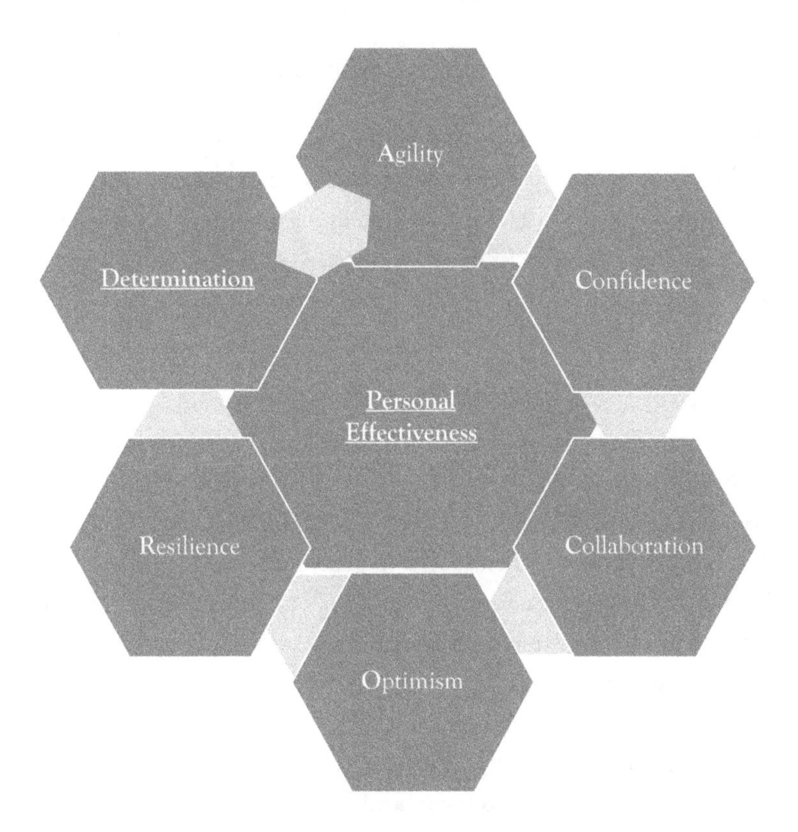

Determination is key to staying personally effective. As discussed earlier when we explored maintaining a realistic perspective, no matter how resilient we are, we are all bound to encounter some professional situations where our efforts—as well as our end results—can really miss the mark. Oftentimes, this can elicit varying degrees of disappointment, disillusionment, and highly undesirable feelings of discouragement.

In these cases, discouragement, while perhaps the most common-sounding of the three, may actually be the most destructive emotional reaction. This is because—if not kept in check—*discouragement can often consume not only our physical energy, but the vital drive and motivation needed to keep the kind of forward focus that is required to maintain our personal and overall efficacy.* **Thus, even more so than with resilience, it is critically important for us to not get "stuck" or stymied by discouragement, no matter how daunting any particular situation may appear at the time.**

In order to ensure that we can keep our all-important energy and motivation, determination is key.

Components of Determination

For our final element of ACCORD, we will explore how focus, self-leadership, and patient persistence can not only underpin but proactively fuel our determination, helping to repeatedly propel us forward through setbacks of all kinds.

Focus

We have looked at the importance of focus in a more general sense throughout this book, as it can assist us in so many ways in our pursuit of desirable outcomes for all of our work. After all, distraction has tremendous potential to sideline even the best-laid plans and efforts, and in the 21st century, it can be rather foolish to pretend that any one of us is truly immune to it. Various and numerous types of undesirable stimuli—not the least of which are residual feelings of professional inadequacy that can resurface, even after we have mastered a good degree of resilience—pose a threat to our day-to-day productivity, and efficacy.

So here, in order to help us master determination, we want to take a very specific approach to focus, and acknowledge the need for it in direct relation to being and staying determined.

Think of them as symbiotic entities like the flowers and bees, in that one will always need the other to flourish.

This does not mean that we necessarily need to gloss over and\or try to invalidate our feelings. Simply let them be, and know them for the authentic emotional reactions that they are. Choose to process them in a healthful manner for yourself, and those around you. Enlist help—personal or professional—if needed.

Then, be sure to choose reflection over rumination, with an eye to benefitting from the learning gathered from any setbacks or mistakes. Avoid marinating in any psychic haze that may be lingering around the imperfect outcome itself. Consciously acknowledge that you, as a human being, are not the outcome and, while you may have invested considerable work toward it, know that an outcome is a thing, separate and apart from yourself.

All of the aforementioned should begin to lay a sturdy-enough groundwork required for regaining the degree of focus needed to fuel true determination. When ready to move toward the desired outcome again, and as with being resilient, take as many steps back and deep breaths as are needed to help shake off any lingering negative feelings. Then, engage with renewed vigor in all those positive and purposeful activities that are required to achieve what needs to happen next. As a valid and thinking human being, acknowledge that you can now readdress the task involved with greater knowledge and experience.

Start with small steps if needed, but even then, infuse them with energy and optimism. Revisit lessons learned on an ongoing basis, and as touched upon in previous sections, act on that learning with an open mind, the kind of confidence gained from experience, and genuine resolve. Keep a focused eye on the prize. If a visual aid can assist your mind's eye, imagine that—as with the powerful legs of the kangaroo—you are only able to jump forward. Try to do so with all the positive intentions and beneficial energy you can muster, as that should serve to fuel your focus and resultant determination even more, and in the best way possible.

Self-Leadership

However much we may look up to our leaders, and no matter how exemplary their leadership has been in the past, we must strive to keep in mind that like us, they are only human beings. Thus, they are subject to vacillating, and even sometimes truly erratic behaviors—especially in times of challenge and change.

Much to our dismay, we have all probably witnessed our formerly stoic and capable bosses crumble into an assortment of odd and sometimes even off-putting actions and reactions when they are faced with stress—especially the kind of unprecedented types of stress most of us have experienced at our current point in history.[1] Understandably, we may want nothing more than for them to go back to whatever our expectation of normalcy is from them. Oftentimes, we do what we can to try to prop them back up and point them in what we perceive to be the right direction.

But realistically, there is not much one adult can do to modify the behavior of another adult, unless that modification is something that the other party has requested or volunteered for. This can be especially true of those whom we report to, as particularly when under stress, it may be natural for a supervisor of any kind to try and double down on keeping up a veneer of competency and command—even while their actions are visibly and sorely betraying that intent.

So, while we generally cannot change the behavior of our supervisors, we certainly can modify the way we respond to them—and the situations they may be struggling through—to solicit a more positive outcome for everyone.

This requires self-leadership, even for those of us who have always thought of ourselves more as dutiful followers for most or all of our working lives.

And what does self-leadership mean, in a very concrete sense, to be applied to what needs to be done to remain effective in through these kinds of challenges?

First, we can find some grounding by drawing upon everything we have learned so far about agility, confidence, collaboration, optimism, resilience, and what we now know about very consciously and specifically applying focus in the interest of determination. And, if we are leaders in any context at all—such as performing the lead in a choir or coaching a swim team—we can also draw upon the sense of satisfaction that we get from perhaps not always taking home the trophy, but knowing that we put our best foot forward not only for ourselves, but for others, as well.

Importantly, we want to focus on *mindfully responding* to each situation, as opposed to simply reacting. Then, we can simply but clearly consider how we would actually want to be led.

A simple exercise to that end is provided here.

Preparing for Self-Leadership: An Exercise

1. Start by thinking about the next time you look in the mirror, staying unconcerned about the physicality of your reflection, but clearly seeing the way the person there (you) embodies all the most admirable elements of your character.

2. Focus specifically and exclusively on the good. Know that you can self-lead in a way that not only supports those resultant good feelings, but will serve to bring them back time and again.
3. Exercise confidence in knowing that you can proceed in a manner that is genuinely true to your very best self. If given the opportunity to lead others, know that you can do the same in those instances.
4. Keep in mind that for effective self-leadership, it is critical to do everything possible to maintain—and, ideally, elevate—our own behavioral standards. We can choose to employ best practices while we self-lead, when those we report to are falling short in that arena.
5. Remember that kindness, fairness, and patience all matter, and by and large, it can be advisable—especially when under stress—to apply all three of those qualities to ourselves, as well.

Now that we are better prepared to do so, let us next identify some behaviors that can help us achieve and maintain effective self-leadership.

Self-Leadership Behaviors

- **Applying meaningful, positive values, while also exercising sound judgment.** The famed business guru and educator Peter Drucker said: "Management is doing things right; leadership is doing the right things."[2] Especially when presented with a choice that affects others, honor your values and take the high road to the most mutually beneficial solution or next step possible. It is understood that in more tenuous situations, this may feel like an exercise in choosing the proverbial "lesser of two evils." In cases like that, strive to always do the absolute best that you can, with what you have to work with. If conflicted about it, consider that this may not only help you sleep better at night, but if the situation ever comes under scrutiny, it will be clear that you put your best foot forward for yourself, and any other parties that could have been impacted.

- **Knowing your true strengths, and capitalizing on them whenever the opportunity presents itself.** For many of us, it can be somewhat natural to cast a critical eye upon oneself. Because of that, knowing our weaknesses may come to us rather easily, while identifying what our true strengths are can be a bit more difficult. There is a wealth of information written on the subject, in all kinds of formats, to suit all kinds of audiences. To help us get a running start on the subject, a brief exercise is provided later, intended to assist those of us that have a tougher time appreciating our natural gifts, as well as our developed talents and accomplishments.
- **Respecting your own emotions, while endeavoring to act kindly, fairly, and objectively**. Remember what we said about validation? The way you feel about how you or your team has been treated matters—acknowledge that. But keep in mind that a cool head and reasonable approach are needed to maintain the vital energy required to maintain true determination, and keep moving things forward. To help with this, again avoid associating any undesirable events or outcomes with specific teams or individuals. In other words, avoid getting pulled into a nonproductive vortex of blame. Maintain focus on the desirable outcome, further to what was discussed about keeping a results orientation, under Resilience. It is far more advisable to take a step back, depersonalize the situation, and think in terms of upcoming milestones and results, as opposed to fixating on any past missteps—including your own. It is not suggested to ignore reality, as the reality of a positive and desirable result is what we are after. Just keep in mind that kindness, fairness, and objectivity can very much apply to self-reflection, as well.

As referenced, the next exercise is provided to help us boost our self-leadership capabilities by identifying our strengths. From there, we can, ideally, put them to their best use.

Knowing Your Strengths Exercise

All this activity requires is a quiet space, a copy of your resume, and your list of job references. Optionally, make your LinkedIn profile available, as well, if you have one.

a. First, do what you can to truly quiet your mind—get out of your own head, as they say.
b. Next, assume the role of someone who is hiring for an opportunity that you could be suited for. Then, review your resume with the perspective of someone who does not know you at all, and who has never seen the resume before. At the same time, keep up a conscious effort to, again, stay out of one's own head. *But why would we use a resume, here?* As we have learned to highlight our strengths and accomplishments on our CVs, they should provide easy access to a fairly concise list of things we have done well.
c. Then, again with the eye of someone looking for a candidate with your type of background, take a moment to consider and appreciate all the knowledge, skills, and abilities required to achieve those accomplishments you have listed. No matter what chronological stage your career is at, be sure to consider all of the hard work, education, motivation, positive attributes, and quality experience that have been necessary for this candidate (you) to get to this current point in time. Take some time to genuinely respect and value all of that about yourself.
d. Next, review your reference list, taking note of everyone on it. Reflect upon all of the good reasons that the people on that list have made themselves available to support your professional prospects. Here again, take enough time to mindfully acknowledge some of the positive things they would say about you.

e. You can stop here, if you like—just be sure to fully recognize your strengths in a very conscious manner before moving on to the next thing. But, if available, you may also find it helpful to take a look at any endorsements or accolades received on LinkedIn or other preferred social media outlet that you use for business. This, too, can help you to objectively identify and appreciate all those things that you are really good at—your true and quite valuable strengths.

Patient Persistence

When we think of persistence, a certain degree of patience is implicit, at least for most of us. The necessity to apply and then reapply oneself repeatedly and effectively to a particular goal requires sustained composure, as well as a degree of fortitude that can correlate pretty directly with the degree of effort involved in achieving a desired outcome.

Most of us have now learned that it can be quite beneficial to approach a specific objective or enter into a worthwhile project having first identified how laborious the endeavor will be. However, we may have also discovered that over time, this is simply not always possible, given all the variables that endeavor could encompass. As one milestone is victoriously achieved, it can be relatively common for that victory to unearth new challenges, as discussed throughout much of this book, and covered in some detail in our section titled "Planned Pragmatism."

Thus, know that patience is not only considered a virtue, but also seems rather indispensable to staying personally effective, especially as it applies to the necessity for persistence in much of what needs to happen in order to achieve our goals.

This is not always easily done, especially if you live or work in a culture that worships speed above all else. In such cases, remember that "to persist" implies continuous action, and consider that even a race car driver must rely heavily on the patience and persistence of the engineers who designed the vehicle itself, in order to have an optimal advantage at race time. This does not compel the driver to slow down. On the contrary, the rigorously composed product of a good design team can facilitate the increased probability of winning that race, despite any obstacles that may arise along the way, and in a manner that is as safe as possible, all things considered.

If it does not come naturally to you, what we learned under "Balanced Lifestyle and Self-Care" can assist in cultivating a sense of patience. Suggestions provided around downtime as a routine, choosing happiness, practicing gratitude, and getting quality rest may be especially helpful. Draw upon all of what has been discussed so far to resume activities, or perhaps even ascertain that it is more beneficial to restart at the beginning. Consciously exercise an authentic willingness to review and start anew as many times as is required—no less, but no more, either. Having achieved a good degree of personal efficacy, you will know when it is actually time to stop. Be ready to devote (and manage) whatever time is necessary to tend to the detailed planning up front, as we can again reference in our example in the "Adaptability" section. Doing so may lessen the potential for needed "fixes" later on, while increasing the potential for greater success, overall.

Summing Up

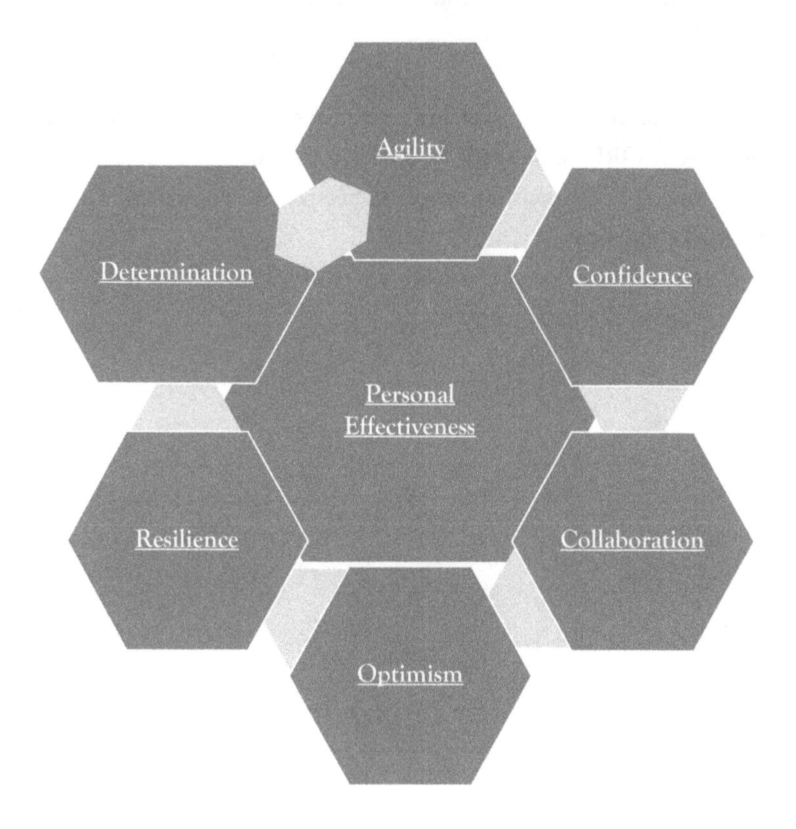

In sum, leverage all of the previous five elements to master chaos through ACCORD:

- Agility, to adapt to a revised role or project, or simply a new approach
- Confidence, to draw upon experience and illuminate all embedded wins
- Collaboration, to support progress, employing the team's collective talents and intellectual capital
- Optimism, to keep energy levels high and progress marching forward

- Resilience, which is now reinforced through further learning and experience
- Determination, underpinning the ability to navigate demanding situations and overcome the most stubborn of obstacles

Then, of course—as evolving circumstances will usually dictate—revisit ACCORD as needed, in order to provide a bit more wind at your back, while exercising personal effectiveness through all kinds of workaday challenges.

Here's wishing our readers much success in the pursuit of all things positive, and, of course, personally effective!

Notes

Element One

1. Vozza (2017).
2. Manoukian (2016).
3. Ghandi (n.d.).
4. Seneca (n.d.).

Element Two

1. Rodin (n.d.).
2. Edison (n.d.).
3. Weisman (2012).
4. Patel (2015).
5. Sarwar (2018).
6. Weisman (2012).

Element Three

1. Lowenbraun (n.d.).
2. Wilingham (2012).
3. Oxford Advanced Learner's Dictionary (n.d.).
4. Recruiting Daily Advisor Editorial Staff (2018).
5. Merriam-Webster, Merriam-Webster Dictionary (n.d.).

Element Four

1. Angelou (n.d.).
2. Duignan (2021).

Element Five

1. Cambridge Advanced Learner's Dictionary and Thesaurus (n.d.).
2. Szalavitz (2012).

Element Six

1. Mautz (2019).
2. "Peter F. Drucker Quotes." (2021).

References

"Peter F. Drucker > Quotes." n.d. *goodreads*. www.goodreads.com/author/quotes/12008.Peter_F_Drucker.

Angelou, M. n.d. "Shadow Sayings and Quotes." Wisesayings.com. www.wisesayings.com/shadow-quotes/.

Cambridge Advanced Learner's Dictionary and Thesaurus. n.d. "Mindfulness." *Cambridge Dictionary*. Cambridge University Press. https://dictionary.cambridge.org/us/dictionary/english/mindfulness.

Duignan, B. May 28, 2021. "Occam's Razor." *Encyclopedia Britannica*. www.britannica.com/topic/Occams-razor.

Edison, T.A. n.d "Thomas A. Edison." *Quotespedia*. www.quotespedia.org/authors/t/thomas-a-edison/i-have-not-failed-ive-just-found-10000-ways-that-wont-work-thomas-a-edison/.

Ghandi, M. n.d. "Mahatma Ghandi." *Quotespedia*. www.quotespedia.org/authors/m/mahatma-gandhi/be-the-change-that-you-wish-to-see-in-the-world-mahatma-gandhi/.

Lowenbraun, N. n.d. "Facial Expressions Matter When Presenting Here's Why." *Duarte*. www.duarte.com/presentation-skills-resources/facial-expressions-matter-when-presenting-heres-why/.

Manoukian, J.G. September 29, 2016. "Risk Appetite and Risk Tolerance: What's the Difference?" *Wolters Kluwer*. www.wolterskluwer.com/en/expert-insights/risk-appetite-and-risk-tolerance-whats-the-difference.

Mautz, S. February 21, 2019. "Want to Improve Your Style Under Stress? New Research Shows You How." *Inc*. www.inc.com/scott-mautz/new-research-shows-how-you-lead-under-stress-has-a-bigger-impact-than-you-thought-heres-how-to-get-it-right.html.

Merriam-Webster, Merriam-Webster Dictionary. n.d. "Influence (noun)." Merriam-Webster.com. www.merriam-webster.com/dictionary/influence.

Oxford Advanced Learner's Dictionary. n.d. "Validation *Noun*." *Oxford Learner's Dictionaries*. Oxford University Press. www.oxfordlearnersdictionaries.com/us/definition/english/validation#:~:text=%2F%CB%8Cv%C3%A6l%C9%AA%CB%88de%C9%AA%CA%83n%2F,%2F%CB%8Cv%C3%A6l%C9%AA%CB%88de%C9%AA%CA%83n%2F,something%20is%20true%20or%20correct.

Patel, S. August 31, 2015. "10 People Who Became Wildly Successful After Facing Rejection." www.entrepreneur.com/article/249961.

Recruiting Daily Advisor Editorial Staff. January 29, 2018. "4 Tips to Combat the High Cost of Employee Disengagement." *HR Daily Advisor.* https://hrdailyadvisor.blr.com/2018/01/29/4-tips-combat-high-cost-employee-disengagement/.

Rodin, A. n.d. "Auguste Rodin Quotes." *BrainyQuote.* www.brainyquote.com/quotes/auguste_rodin_105026.

Sarwar, H. September 4, 2018. "Bill Gates 1st startup Traf-O-Data Was a failure in 70s–Failure Is Just a Word If You Look Back at Your Mistakes." *being GURU.* www.beingguru.com/2018/09/bill-gates-1st-startup-traf-o-data-was-a-failure-in-70s-failure-is-just-a-word-if-you-look-back-at-your-mistakes/.

Seneca. n.d. "Seneca Quotes." Goodreads.com. www.goodreads.com/quotes/409452-the-fates-lead-those-who-will-those-who-won-t-they.

Szalavitz, M. January 11, 2012. "Q&A: Jon Kabat-Zinn Talks About Bringing Mindfulness Meditation to Medicine." *Time.* https://healthland.time.com/2012/01/11/mind-reading-jon-kabat-zinn-talks-about-bringing-mindfulness-meditation-to-medicine/.

Vozza, S. November 14, 2017. "4 Ways to Train Your Brain to Be More Open-Minded." *Fast Company.* www.fastcompany.com/40494077/4-ways-to-train-your-brain-to-be-more-open-minded.

Weisman, A. October 29, 2012. "15 People Who Became Wildly Successful After Facing Rejection." *Business Insider.* www.businessinsider.com/15-people-who-failed-before-becoming-famous-2012-10#oprah-winfrey-was-told-she-was-unfit-for-tv-3.

Weisman, A. October 29, 2012. "15 People Who Failed Before Becoming Famous." *Business Insider.* www.businessinsider.com/15-people-who-failed-before-becoming-famous-2012-10#walt-disney-was-told-a-mouse-would-never-work-1.

Wilingham, E. October 16, 2012. "Low Eye Contact Is Not Just an Autism Thing." *Forbes.* www.forbes.com/sites/emilywillingham/2012/10/16/low-eye-contact-is-not-just-an-autism-thing/?sh=7825d6297f5c.

About the Author

Lucia Strazzeri has more than 20 years of experience in human resources and organizational development, facilitating success among work groups ranging from the shop floor through technical and scientific teams, all the way to the C-suite. She has held numerous consultative and leadership roles in her field, serving as a primary organizational development and performance management resource for international and domestic companies of all sizes. Lucia holds SPHR and SHRM-SCP industry certifications, as well as an MS in human resources from Fordham University.

Index

OTHER TITLES IN THE HUMAN RESOURCE MANAGEMENT AND ORGANIZATIONAL BEHAVIOR COLLECTION

Vilma Barr, Consultant, Editor

- *11 Secrets of Nonprofit Excellence* by Kathleen Stauffer
- *The Nonprofit Imagineers* by Ben Vorspan
- *At Home With Work* by Nyla Naseer
- *Improv to Improve Your Leadership Team* by Candy Campbell
- *Leadership In Disruptive Times* by Sattar Bawany
- *The Intrapreneurship Formula* by Sandra Lam
- *Navigating Conflict* by Lynne Curry
- *Innovation Soup* by Sanjay Puligadda and Don Waisanen
- *The Aperture for Modern CEOs* by Sylvana Storey
- *The Future of Human Resources* by Tim Baker
- *Change Fatigue Revisited* by Richard Dool and Tahsin I. Alam
- *Championing the Cause of Leadership* by Ted Meyer
- *Embracing Ambiguity* by Michael Edmondson
- *Breaking the Proactive Paradox* by Tim Baker
- *The Modern Trusted Advisor* by Nancy MacKay and Alan Weiss

Concise and Applied Business Books

The Collection listed above is one of 30 business subject collections that Business Expert Press has grown to make BEP a premiere publisher of print and digital books. Our concise and applied books are for…

- Professionals and Practitioners
- Faculty who adopt our books for courses
- Librarians who know that BEP's Digital Libraries are a unique way to offer students ebooks to download, not restricted with any digital rights management
- Executive Training Course Leaders
- Business Seminar Organizers

Business Expert Press books are for anyone who needs to dig deeper on business ideas, goals, and solutions to everyday problems. Whether one print book, one ebook, or buying a digital library of 110 ebooks, we remain the affordable and smart way to be business smart. For more information, please visit www.businessexpertpress.com, or contact sales@businessexpertpress.com.

Printed in the USA
CPSIA information can be obtained
at www.ICGtesting.com
LVHW051143021123
762339LV00010B/148